Alexander Sutherland

**A Summer in Prairie-Land**

2nd Edition

Alexander Sutherland

**A Summer in Prairie-Land**
*2nd Edition*

ISBN/EAN: 9783744679060

Printed in Europe, USA, Canada, Australia, Japan

Cover: Foto ©Thomas Meinert / pixelio.de

More available books at **www.hansebooks.com**

*A SUMMER IN PRAIRIE-LAND.*

# NOTES OF A TOUR

### THROUGH THE

# NORTH-WEST TERRITORY.

BY
## REV. A. SUTHERLAND, D.D.

*SECOND EDITION.*

TORONTO:
PRINTED FOR THE AUTHOR, AT THE METHODIST BOOK AND PUBLISHING HOUSE,
78 & 80 KING STREET EAST.

1882.

# PREFATORY.

ANY eyes from many lands, are looking toward the praries of the great North-West. That this grand Territory is destined to be the home of prosperous millions in the near future, is now all but universally conceded, and hence every item of reliable information in regard to its capabilities and resources is eagerly welcomed./ The causes of this wide-spread interest are various. Speculators look to the North-West as a promising place for investments, where large returns may be secured without work, and at small outlay; the Micawbers of society regard it as a place where "something" is likely to "turn up," and seldom discover their mistake till they themselves are turned down; impecunious politicians look fondly toward it as a land

where " virtue," invisible at home, shall find—
not be—"its own reward," and where services
to the "party" shall be recompensed by a good
fat berth at the people's expense; political
" prophets," tired of living " without honour "
in " their own country," prepare to seek in the
North-West a more appreciative constituency,
where some favoring breeze may waft them
into that desired haven—a seat in parliament;
while projectors and builders of railways, as
they turn their gaze toward the setting sun,
behold saleable charters and fat contracts
stretching out in endless perspective, and bless
their stars that " the [railway] lines " have at
last " fallen unto them in pleasant places."

In contributing my quota to the general
stock of information in regard to the North-
West, I design it for classes very different
from those just mentioned. I have in view
the interests of struggling thousands in the
overcrowded countries of the Old World, who,
were they once transferred to these fertile
plains, would soon work their way to a manly
independence, and become an invaluable ele-
ment in the society of the future; I am
thinking of the many in the older provinces

of the Dominion who, with stalwart sons growing up around them, are looking for an opportunity to do something for "the boys," to help them to a start in life ; and last, but not least, I am thinking of the churches of the land, who are just beginning to wake up to the fact that they have now before them one of those grand opportunities which may not occur again in the world's history—the opportunity of working out the problem of a Christian civilization on a purely virgin soil; and I would fain present such information as may be, in some degree, helpful to each and all of these.

Part of what is contained in the following pages appeared during the past summer in the correspondence columns of the *Christian Guardian*. The letters, as published, have been carefully revised, the remainder of the series completed, and the whole presented in the chapters which follow. Their publication in this form is in response to requests from many persons who desire to have the information in a shape more permanent than the columns of a newspaper would allow.

It will readily be observed that in some parts of the volume considerable space is occupied with accounts of certain Missions of the Methodist Church, especially among the Indians of the Upper Saskatchewan region. As the main object of my tour was to inspect these missions, and to prospect with reference to the religious needs of the country, extended reference to Mission work was unavoidable; but it is believed that this kind of information will not be unacceptable to those who have the best interests of the country at heart.

A. S.

Toronto, March 25th, 1881.

# CONTENTS.

*Contents.*

# Contents. ix

*Contents.*

## LIST OF ILLUSTRATIONS.

# A SUMMER IN PRAIRIE-LAND.

## I.

### ON THE WAY.

ESIRING, at the outset, to establish confidential relations with the reader, I may state briefly the object with which the tour herein chronicled was undertaken. As Secretary of the Missionary Society of the Methodist Church, part of my duty is to become familiar by official correspondence, and personal visitation, when practicable, with the various parts of the Mission field; and as it was probable there would be a demand, at an early day, for the extension of Mission-work in the North-West, I was instructed by the Committee to proceed to that region for the purpose of inspecting existing Missions, and reporting on the probable needs of the near future.

1

There are two routes by either of which the traveller may proceed to the great North-West. Starting
from Toronto, one may go by way of the Lakes as far
as Duluth, at the extreme westerly point of Lake
Superior, and from thence westward by the Northern
Pacific; or, if time be an object, he may go by rail,
*via* Chicago and St. Paul, intersecting route No. 1 at
Brainerd or Glyndon. From the latter point the traveller has again the choice of two routes : he may turn
directly northward, by the St. Paul and Manitoba
Railway, and enter the country at Emerson ; or, keeping on the line of the Northern Pacific Railway, he
may go westward, through the territories of Dakota
and Montana, enter Canadian territory a hundred
miles east of the Rocky Mountains, proceed northward
as far as he wishes to go, and then strike east and
south-east, coming out by way of Manitoba, and so
on, as the surveyors say, "to the place of beginning."
For various reasons I chose the latter route, and it is
of this tour, and of what I saw and heard, that I now
propose to give some little account. After some consultation I decided to join the Rev. John McDougall,
who was about returning from Ontario, with a band of
missionaries and teachers, to his work in the Saskatchewan District, as I would thus have the advantage of travelling, for a considerable distance at least,
with one thoroughly familiar with the routes and with
the modes of travel which the state of the country
rendered necessary.

The Mission party left Toronto on the 17th of June,

taking the rout by Collingwood and Duluth, while, to economize time, I remained at the office a few days longer, and then proceeded by rail, *via* Chicago and St. Paul. The heat was very great, and the dust at times excessive, and matters got worse as we sped westward, till at St. Paul the climax was reached in an atmosphere that was fairly stifling. A learned St. Paulician made some wise observations about the mean temperature of the State. The aptness of the phrase struck me at once : it was the "meanest" temperature I had experienced in ten years. Toward evening of the 23rd a heavy hail and thunder storm that came up from the westward cleared and cooled the atmosphere, so that I left St. Paul in comparative comfort, and with a far kindlier feeling toward the inhabitants than when I entered it. So largely are our feelings shaped by circumstances.

Twelve hours in St. Paul gave ample opportunity to provide some necessaries for the long journey which lay before me. In the evening I took the St. Paul and Pacific line for Brainerd, expecting to con-nect at that point with the train bringing the Mission party from Duluth. Sinking back in the comfortable seat, I prepared to "rest and be thankful," while gazing dreamily on the swiftly-changing panorama of village, and homestead, and open prairie. Oddly enough, the first thing that fairly arrested my atten-tion was the ubiquitous "railway dog," to be seen on some part of every line in the country, who conceives that the great end of life is to beat the railway train—

if he can.  Yonder he comes from the nearest farm-house, helter skelter over "field and fallow," head down, tail streaming out behind ; first at right angles with the train, as if bound to precipitate a collision : then swerving to an angle of forty-five, as if to outwit the enemy by a flank movement ; then falling into a parallel line he settles down to his work with an air that says, "You may be big, but it's muscle that tells !" Idle boast ! Muscle has no chance in competition with steam.  For a few rods he holds on with *dogged* resolution, though drifting hopelessly to the rear ; then realizing for the hundreth time that it's a lost race, he suddenly stops, wheels round, and with "arms reversed," or, to discard metaphor, with drooping tail, plods sadly homeward, meditating on the vanity of doggish aspirations, and, untaught by experience, preparing to repeat the futile effort the very next day.  And yet, why should we blame the poor fellow, while thousands of his human brethren daily perpetrate the same folly, and by stubbornly clinging to exploded theories and worn-out ideas, gain no wisdom by experience, and are doomed to perpetual defeat ?  And all the while the indolent passengers on the train calmly contemplate the frantic struggles of the "unlucky dogs," and thank God that they themselves are not as other men are.  But a truce to dogmatics for the present.

> "How soft, how beautiful, comes on
> The stilly hour when storms are gone,"

wrote Tom Moore; and any one who witnessed with us a prairie sunset, after leaving St. Paul on the 23rd, must have appreciated the sentiment. The storm of the afternoon had passed by, and the heavy clouds rolled eastward, spanned by a rainbow of wondrous beauty. In the west a thinner stratum lifted from the horizon, exposing a broad band of clear sky, not brightly blue as in the daytime, but with a soft transparent haze, as if seen through a mist of tears. Soon heavier masses of cloud rolled slowly upward, and ranged themselves against the soft-tinted background, their lower edges straight and symmetrical, their upper edges broken and ragged, and constantly changing into new and strange forms. Now they seemed like massive ramparts, crowned with frowning battlements and towers; now like the domes and spires of a great city, with the grand proportions of a vast cathedral towering high above the whole. Then, as the sun sank toward the horizon, from behind the sombre clouds there suddenly issued a mellow flood of golden splendor, and in a moment rampart and battlement, tower and spire, softened into masses of foliage, crowning isles of Eden-like beauty, anchored in a golden sea; while, as if to complete the illusion, fragments of fleecy vapor went floating by, like stately ships sailing amid those happy islands up to some quiet haven that as yet I could not see. Perhaps the reader will remember how, when travelling by rail or steamer, and gazing upon a swiftly-changing landscape, the half-remembered words of some poet's rhymes went echo-

ing through the chambers of memory, keeping time to
the beat of the paddles, or the clank of the wheels.
Even so, as I gazed, words read long years ago, touched
by some subtle law of association, came back again :—

> "There was a ship one eve autumnal onward
>     Steered o'er an ocean lake,
> Steered by some strong hand ever as if sunward ;
>     Behind, an angry wake ;
> Before, there stretched a sea that grew intenser,
>     With silver fire far spread
> Up to a hill, mist-gloried like a censer,
>     With smoke encompasséd.
> It seemed as if two seas met brink to brink,—
> A silver flood beyond a lake of ink.
>
> There was a soul that eve autumnal sailing
>     Beyond the earth's dark bars,—
> Toward the land of sunsets never paling,
>     Toward heaven's sea of stars.
> Behind, there was a wake of billows tossing ;
>     Before, a glory lay.
> O happy soul, with all sail set, just crossing
>     Into the far away !
> The gleam and gloom, the calmness and the strife,
> Were death before thee, and behind thee life.
>
> And as that ship went up the waters stately,
>     Upon her topmast tall
> I saw two sails, whereof the one was greatly
>     Dark as a funeral pall ;
> But oh ! the next's pure whiteness who shall utter ?
>     Like a shell-snowy strand,
> Or where a sunbeam falleth through the shutter
>     On a dead baby's hand:

Yet both alike, across the surging sea,
Helped to the haven where the bark would be.

And as that soul went onward sweetly speeding
    Unto its home and light,
Repentance made it sorrowful exceeding,
    Faith made it wondrous bright ;
Repentance dark with shadowy recollections,
    And longings unsufficed ;
Faith white and pure with sunniest affections,
    Full from the face of Christ.
Yet both across the sun-besilvered tide
Helped to the haven where the heart would ride."

But as I sat and dreamed there was another change
without ; for daylight sobered into twilight, and twilight gloomed into darkness, and the splendors of that
sunset were gone. Gone where ? Who can tell ?
Perhaps into some eternal storehouse, to be reproduced
again when the Transient becomes the Permanent,
and " this mortal " has " put on immortality." There
is an exquisite little bit of philosophy in the following lines—I cannot recall the author's name—which
may be truer than we know :—

    " This world I deem
    But a beautiful dream
Of shadows that are not what they seem ;
    Whence visions rise,
    Giving dim surmise
Of things that shall greet our waking eyes."

At midnight of the 23rd our car was switched on to
the main line of the Northern Pacific, and attached to
the train from Duluth. On the following morning I

passed into another car and joined the rest of the party, which consists of the Rev. John McDougall, who with his family goes to resume his work at Morley; his mother, wife of our brave Missionary who perished on the plains; Mrs. Sibbald, wife of the teacher at Morley, who goes to rejoin her husband; Rev. John McLean and wife, Missionary to Fort McLeod and the Blackfeet; Mr. Youmans and wife, teacher for Whitefish Lake; Mr. Nelson and wife, teacher for Woodville; and Mr. Glass and wife, teacher for Saddle Lake, a new station where work is to be begun by organizing a school. Besides these, there are some relatives of Mrs. McDougall, who propose seeking a home in the far west; Miss A., of Cobourg, who seeks a year's rest and recuperation; and my old friend, R. Warren, Esq., of Niagara, who hopes—I think on good grounds—to profit much in his physical man by taking the round trip. Altogether, we form quite a company for mutual protection and help.

During nearly the whole of the 24th our route lay through the Territory of Dakota, which may be described as one vast prairie. For hours together we sped onward without seeing tree, bush, or shrub to break the monotony; nothing to bound the view but the distant horizon. We passed very few streams, and these not large; but small lakes were tolerably numerous, and where the land had been broken up and cultivated, it seemed to be fertile. We passed through several of the monster wheat farms, that have been so often described. One of these, the Cass-

Cheney farm, comprises some 50,000 acres, of which over 8,000 have already been brought under cultivation, and more is being rapidly prepared. Another, the Steele farm, presented unbroken wheat fields on either side of the track, extending for several miles, and the crop looked remarkably healthy. But time is required to tell whether the other parts of the Territory will be equally productive, and whether there is moisture enough to insure a regular crop. And time will tell another thing, namely, the disastrous effect upon a country's development and prosperity of these huge monopolies.

At Bismarck our railway journey ended, and here we found there would be no boat up the Missouri River for several days. We have very comfortable quarters, however, at the Sheridan House, which is owned, I believe, by the Railway Company, and here I suppose we must remain till the boat is ready to go—a disappointment to the whole party, who are anxious to push on.

## II.

## UP THE MISSOURI.

" To the West, to the West, to the land of the free,
  Where the *muddy* Missouri rolls down to the sea."

HE poet wrote "mighty;" but "muddy" has
more truth in it, if less poetry.   Of all the
muddy streams I ever saw, this is the muddiest—worse than the Don or the Humber
at Toronto.   And we are likely to see a good
deal of it, for there is a trip of 1,200 miles
ahead of us before we reach Fort Benton, the head
of river navigation.

As before mentioned, we had an annoying delay at
Bismarck.   Mr. McDougall and party had taken
through tickets to Fort Benton, being assured of close
connections at the various points.   From Duluth a
despatch was sent to Bismarck, inquiring when a
steamer would leave for Benton, and the agent of the
Collingwood boats at Duluth reported, as answer, that
a boat would leave Bismarck on the 25th of June.

Accordingly the party pushed on, and reached Bismarck on the evening of the 24th. Here we found two boats of the line, but the Agent was at Cincinnati, attending the Democratic Convention, and neither of the boats could be freighted till his return; nor did any one know which of the two boats would go to Benton, consequently we could not go on board. There was nothing for it but to go to a hotel and wait. Had the success of the Democratic candidate depended on the Mission party, his chances would have been poor. We heartily wished him and his Convention

"Anywhere, anywhere, out of the world."

On Sunday morning we made our way to the little hall where the Methodist Society worships, and Bro. McLean discoursed earnestly from " We will go with you, for we have heard that God is with you," after which most of the party turned in and assisted in the Sunday-school. In the evening I proclaimed Christ " mighty to save," and we closed the day with an old-fashioned class-meeting, many feeling and saying, " It is good to be here." On the following Tuesday evening I preached by invitation in the Presbyterian church to a small but attentive audience. There is need for all possible Christian effort in these frontier towns. Bismarck is a place of, I should suppose, some 2,000 people, and I am told there are—or were—in it sixty whisky and gambling saloons. The Methodist pastor is doing a good work in the Temperance reform, some four or five hundred having joined the Red

Ribbon movement through his efforts.   His noble wife co-operates heartily in every good work.

The steamboat agent returned from Cincinnati on Monday evening, decided which boat should go to Benton, and made arrangements for us to go on board the next morning.  He kindly offered to send an omnibus to take the party to the steamboat landing, some two miles off, but, like the "heathen Chinee," these western steamboat agents are "peculiar," for after sending those who wished to ride to the boat, he refused to foot the bill, and wanted to throw it back on the party.   We emphatically declined, claiming that we had through tickets.   He attempted to repudiate the through ticket arrangement, even going so far as to say that he had a telegram from Mr. Cumberland, of Toronto, stating that he had not promised the party close connections.   Finally, I believe, the claim of the 'bus driver was settled by the captain or purser of the boat.   It will be well for others who may contemplate taking this route to the North-West to be very definite in their arrangements with regard to through tickets.

It is remarkable how one will, when travelling, stumble upon old acquaintances, or acquaintances of acquaintances, in the most unlikely places.   I found that the agent of the Northern Pacific Railway at Bismarck was a Scotchman named Davidson, who formerly lived at Berlin, and was at one time Deputy Sheriff of the County of Waterloo.   He was acquainted (not *officially*, I beg it to be understood) with many of my

old friends in and about Guelph ; and he gave our
party a good deal of assistance in getting luggage, &c.,
to the boat.  A Mr. McNider, also from Canada, intro-
duced himself, and on Tuesday kindly took Bro. McD.
and myself for a drive in and about Bismarck.  His
partner is a Mr. McLean, from Souris, P. E. I., and his
book-keeper, a Mr. Snodgrass, is from the country
back of Port Hope.  Our drive took us down to the
river bottoms, and around a four-hundred acre field of
wheat belonging to Mr. McNider.  It is a sight worth
seeing.  Almost the entire field is as level as a floor,
and the wheat appears to be in first-class condition.
Last year Mr. McNider raised 22,000 bushels of oats,
which sold readily at fifty cents a bushel.  As we
drove along, my kind acquaintance pointed out a
number of houses occupied by Highlanders from the
country back of Cornwall, and others occupied by
Nova Scotians.  I am surprised at the number of
Canadians out here.

At 2 a.m. on Dominion Day we got away from
Bismarck, to our great relief.  Up the Missouri the
scenery is pleasant, though not very varied.  The
water is rather above the usual height, and the stream
would average fully a mile in width during the
distance travelled the first two days; and this, be it
remembered, is more than 1,500 miles from its mouth.
The banks, for long distances, preserve the same
general character—alluvial bottoms, covered with
a growth of ash and cotton-wood; and beyond these
naked bluffs, rising at intervals from 50 to 200 feet

in height, their faces deeply channeled by rains and laid bare by enormous land slides. The water steadily undermines the soft friable banks, and vast masses of earth are continually toppling in, mingling with the current, giving the water the consistency, and more than the colour, of pea soup; and as this is the only water for drinking, a good set of teeth, for straining purposes, would seem to be indispensable. Still, when filtered, or the mud allowed to settle, the water is by no means unpalatable.

Being loyally inclined, we thought it a pity to let Dominion Day pass without recognition, so in the evening, a celebration was extemporised, consisting of singing, readings and recitations, concluding with a stanza of " God Save the Queen."

Our experience of sharp practice was not yet ended. We had not proceeded very far up the river when a sable porter put in an appearance, and proceeded to put checks on a number of trunks that had been piled on the forward deck. He then approached one of our party and suavely observed,—

" Fifty cents for each trunk, sah."

" For what ? " was asked.

" For porterage, sah."

" For porterage ! Are you going to put them in the baggage room ? "

" No, sah ; jes' leave 'em whar dey is, sah."

" Now, will you just explain the precise advantage of putting checks on these trunks ? "

" Well, de trunks might get lost, sah."

"Not *very* likely; our trunks are not inclined to somnambulism; they don't walk in their sleep; and as they are on the upper deck, it isn't likely the stokers will mistake them for firewood."

"But we allus puts on checks on dis boat, sah."

"Do you really? Now the only check that's wanted is a check on your impudence, and that had better be put on without unnecessary delay!"

This bit of advice being accompanied by a significant gesture towards the side of the boat, was very impressive, and the "man and brother" retired. This was the end of the check business.

With the exception of this little attempt at extortion, we find things pleasant enough. The captain, purser, pilots, &c., are courteous, the crew quiet, and there is an almost entire absence of that "roughness" which I had always associated with the belongings of a Missouri "flat." So far (I write this when the trip is nearly half over), I have heard few profane words from either officers or men.

On the steamer there is a large quantity of freight, and about twenty passengers besides our own party. Among them is a German from Michigan, going out to Helena, Montana. He chats pleasantly of experiences past and present. Said he,

"When I comes to New York I haf a wife and two schildren, and only five tollar in my pocket. I tell you I haf to work hard; but I likes de country. In Scharmany you darsn't say nodings vat you dinks; but in dis country you can tell any man, *even a b'leeceman* if you dinks he does wrong."

" How did you happen to go to Michigan ?" I asked.

" Vell, I goes first to Chicago, und it vas only a pig mudhole, and everybody haf de ague ; so I goes over near St. Jo in Michigan, and I likes de country, and I gets fifty acres of land. Dere vas plenty of work, but dere vas no money. You haf to take him in provision or shtore. One man tell me if I work for him a while he gif me money enough to buy a cow ; but at dot time cows vas scheep."

" I suppose," I said, " everything was cheap in those days ? "

" Yaas ; I buy a pair of boots for one tollar ; pork vas one tollar and fifty cents a hundred ; and flour vas tree tollars a bar'l. Yaas, everything vas scheep."

" And what do you think of doing in Montana ?"

" Vell, I haf a broder dere dat I hafn't seen for twenty year. I goes out and sees de country, and if I likes him, my vife and poys comes out too."

" So you don't think of going back to Germany ?"

" *No !* only may be for a visit. Dere's too many peoples dare, and "—coming back to the main grievance—" *you darsn't say nodings vat you dinks.*"

During the day we passed Fort Berthold, near which is an Indian village—a miserable affair. The people belong chiefly to the Mandan tribe, and I should judge are still in their pagan state. Some had on the traditional blanket, a good deal the worse of wear, and very short at one end ; some had garments of as

many colors as Joseph's coat; while one young fellow,
who was helping to gather driftwood from the river,
had on little or nothing besides his birthday dress.

Sunday dawned bright and beautiful. In the forenoon Bro. McDougall preached an earnest discourse
from the words of Gideon's battle-cry ; in the evening
I took charge of the service, which was attended by
all the passengers and a number of the crew. Altogether we spent a pleasant and not unprofitable day.
In the afternoon we passed the mouth of the famous
Yellowstone River, as crooked and dirty as the Missouri.

We do not see so much game in this wild country
as we expected ; but occasionally a deer bounding
through the grass, a beaver sitting on the bank
or diving into the water, or a flock of wild geese
floating with the current, creates a ripple of excitement among those to whom such sights are novelties.

During low water the Missouri is difficult of navigation, owing to its crooked channel and numerous sand
bars; and even at high water there are places where
the pilot has to proceed with caution, and take frequent soundings. Here we are approaching a broad
part of the river, and it is impossible to tell just where
the channel may be, as it oftens changes its location
between one trip and the next. A tap on a bell
near the pilot-house is heard, and a man promptly
takes his stand near the bow with a pole some twelve
feet long in his hand. He plunges the pole into the
water and reports—N-o-o-o Botto-o-o-m !" Again the

2

pole goes down—"Sev-u-u-u-n feet!" A few yards
farther, then another plunge—"Fo-o-o-ur feet!" Once
more—"Thre-e-e-e feet!" and the boat grounds on
the bar. This is probably a common occurrence, for
nobody seems to mind it. Steam is crowded on, the
boat twists and creaks, and soon works its way over
the bar and into deep water again. But sometimes
a spot is reached where there may be only two feet
of water for a short distance, and the boat grounds
firmly. What is to be done? Back down? That is
not in the creed of the Western Yankee. His motto
is emphatically "Go ahead!" On the forward part
of the deck, on either side, there is a strong derrick ;
attached to this is a massive spar, which is swung
over the side and one end dropped to the bottom ;
strong ropes are thrown round the capstan and
attached to a "nigger" engine; steam is turned on;
round goes the capstan ; the ropes run smoothly
through the tackling of the spars, and in a wonderfully short space of time the bow (which is loaded to
draw rather more water than aft) is literally *lifted*
*over* the bar, and away we go again. I had heard of
such a thing as a man lifting himself up by the straps
of his boots; but this was the nearest approach to
the experiment that ever came under my observa-
tion.

On the 5th of July we passed an Indian " Agency,"
where a large number of Sioux were encamped.
Many came down to the landing to see the big "Fire-
canoe." Some were painted and feathered in true

pagan fashion, but nearly all were poorly clothed. We were told that a part of those in the camp had belonged to Sitting Bull's band, and this is quite probable, as we are now less than a hundred miles from the frontier. Many of the men were away up the river hunting buffalo, and a report. had just come in that they had charged a camp of their hereditary enemies, the Crows—whose hunting-grounds are on the other side of the river—and killed twelve men. Amid the motley group on the bank were a number of boys and girls, many of whom, in all probability, had never seen a steamboat before. When the whistle sounded, some took to their heels and ran for their lives, while others, less fearful, stood looking on with true savage wonder, pointing to the mysterious whistle from which the ominous sound—worse than any war-whoop—proceeded. Several of the men came on board the boat, and one of them, resplendent in paint and feathers, walked into the cabin just as a lady of our party was coming out. Instinctively she started back, and her eyes opened rather more widely than usual, whereupon the "noble brave" grinned with intense delight at the impression which his charms had made upon a lady of the Pale Faces.

A BUTTE ON THE UPPER MISSOURI.

## III.

## AMONG THE BUFFALO.

FTER leaving Bismarck we were told that in a day or two we would reach the buffalo country, and might expect to see considerable herds; but as day after day went by and no signs of buffalo appeared, we became skeptical. Entering the cabin one day I found several of the party quietly reading. Walking quickly up to one of them I asked—

"Have you seen the buffalo?"

He started as if he had received a shock from a galvanic battery:

" No!"

"Neither have I. Don't believe there's a single buffalo in all this miserable country."

At this stage of the conversation I found it prudent to retire.

On the sixth day after leaving Bismarck, however, the sight of several drowned animals, floating down the stream, convinced us that there were buffalo somewhere ahead. During the day we counted twenty of these carcases, some floating with the current, some stranded on sand-bars; and as we had only Missouri water to drink we were happy accordingly. but the day passed, and once more we had to turn in without having our eyes gladdened by the sight of a *live* buffalo. We had reached what are called the "Bad Lands" of the Upper Missouri, probably once a lofty and level plateau, but now deeply scored and channeled by the rains and frosts of centuries, forming ranges of steep and lofty hills, very rough and broken, with deep intervening gullies, which to all appearance would scarcely supply pasture for a flock of goats; but it is said the short, scant grass on these hills is very nutritious, and is preferred by the buffalo to the ranker growth on the bottoms. At all events we had ocular demonstration that these animals keep fat on it.

It is hardly necessary to say that the morning of the 7th *dawned*. Most mornings do "dawn," but few people are up in time to see it. My friend Warren was up before the day had fairly dawned, and just as I was indulging in the luxury of a "fresh roll," he put his head in the stateroom doorway and asked—

"Do you want to see them?"

It needed no word to explain what was meant by "*them.*" I got into my clothes with unusual celerity and scrambled up to the pilot-house, and from there got my first glimpse of a herd of buffalo on their native heath. They were half a mile away, but through a glass the individuals of the herd could be distinctly seen, grazing as quietly as a herd of domestic cattle. Word went through the boat, staterooms were quickly vacated, and everybody was on the *qui vive.* Each bend of the river brought us in view of new herds, on both sides, not in dense masses as when migrating, but in scattered bands of from ten to one hundred, sometimes close to the river's bank— from which they went off at a lumbering gallop as the steamer approached. Speculation now began to be rife among the crew as to whether the "Old Man" (*i.e.* the Captain) would allow any shooting to be done, the practice having been forbidden in consequence of several narrow escapes through the careless use of fire-arms in the past. The appearance of the steward, soon after, with a rifle on his arm, indicated that the desired permission had been granted. Quickly several other rifles made their appearance, and all was excitement, though, from the careless handling of some of the weapons, it seemed as though the marksmen would be in greater danger than the game. Attention was now directed to a spot a hundred and fifty yards in advance, where eight or ten dusky forms could be seen, in Indian file, struggling across the current, and we knew it was a band of buffalo swimming the river—a sight of almost hourly occurrence during the rest of the day. The swimmers reached the shore just before we came up with them, but the bank was too steep to climb, and they had to make their way a little farther up stream. Obedient to the pilot's hand on the wheel, the boat swung in toward shore, and in a few moments we were abreast of some six or eight splendid animals, at a distance of not more than ten yards, and getting gradually nearer. Crack went a couple of rifles, and a noble bull came down on his knees, but quickly rose again, and made his way slowly up the steep bank. The boat was now close to shore, and her speed slackened ; a plank was thrust out, and there was a speedy rush and scramble up the bank, a boat hand leading the way and Warren close behind resolved to secure the prize or perish in the attempt. At the same time three other fine bulls rushed past the boat and plunged into the river, but as the motion of the boat was not entirely checked, the bow bumped against the shaggy sides of the struggling animals, who were too much confused to get quickly out of the way. A shot from the lower deck wounded one in the head; and although from the strength of the current it was evident we could not secure him, yet rather than leave him to a lingering death a couple of shots from a Winchester rifle were sent after him, which quickly ended the matter, and after swimming a short distance he gave up the struggle and floated lifeless down the stream. Meanwhile the party who had gone after the wounded bull returned in triumph, dragging the huge beast along by the united strength of twenty pairs of arms. He was soon on board, and at dinner that day roast buffalo was added to our usual bill of fare.

It was now breakfast time, and even buffalo must

not be allowed to interfere with that. It was tacitly agreed that no more shooting should be done, unless to secure a young animal for the table, as it was felt to be wanton cruelty to kill for the mere sake of killing. Breakfast over, all were soon on deck again, watching with unflagging interest the vast numbers of animals to be seen on every side. As we steamed along, a brown object was seen against the dark bank of the river. It proved to be a buffalo calf that had crossed over, and was resting awhile before seeking a convenient place to get up the bank. Again the boat swung in to shore, and several men sprang off in hope of making a capture. The calf remained perfectly still till they laid hold of it, when it suddenly sprang down the bank and into the river, and started to swim vigorously past the boat. A cast was made with a lasso, but missed. Friend Warren was again promplty on hand with a boat pole, which he pressed against the creature's neck and changed its course. A second cast of the rope was more successful, and in a few moments his calfship was hauled safely on board, and consigned to the care of some of the hands in the "regions below." In the course of an hour or so a second capture was made under similar circumstances. In this case it proved to be a female, and decidedly vixenish withal, strongly resenting her capture, and kicking like an army mule at any one who came near her.

One might suppose that shooting two buffaloes and capturing two calves was enough for one day; but

before we go much farther a third calf is sighted,
and as avarice grows by what it feeds on, it is resolved to attempt the capture of this one also.
The bank is steep and lofty, and the calf is en-
sconced on a kind of shelf about twenty feet above
the water. As soon as the boat gets near enough,
half a dozen men spring ashore and scramble up the
bank,—no easy task, for the soft friable clay gives
way under their feet like sand or ashes. But what
are difficulties with such a prize in view? Up they
go! Near the spot where the calf is resting, a huge
boulder of clay stands out from the bank, with a narrow passage behind it. The foremost man, perceiving
this, makes a flank movement, with the evident design of "surrounding" the enemy from the rear. Passing the boulder with a spring, he makes a clutch at
the creature's neck. The calf, who is not so stupid as
it looks, springs to its feet and avoids arrest. The
man, with a desperate effort, seizes it by the leg; the
calf (which I should judge is some four months old)
responds with a roar and a bound, and in an instant
down the bank they go, head over heels, making it
difficult to determine whether the strange-looking
object is a duplicate man,—a sort of Siamese twin,
—or whethea both sections are alike calf. Reaching
the bottom of the bank, the "What-Is-It" resolves
itself into its constituent elements, the calf going
splash into the river, the man saving himself by
sticking knee deep in the tenacious mud. Of course
everybody went into convulsions of laughter. To

the spectators the scene was intensely funny; but it did not seem to afford nearly so mueh amusement to the poor fellow who had so suddenly proved that

> "The best laid schemes o' mice and men
> Gang aft agley."

Meanwhile the liberated calf went sailing composedly down the river, to seek a safer landing place at a more convenient season.

Our day's experience had been, thus far, intensely interesting; but richer fortune was yet in store. As we were approaching a grove of cottonwood on a level bottom, four Indians were seen riding quickly down a neighbouring slope. They disappeared behind the timber, but soon re-appeared on the river bank. All seemed to have good horses, but only one carried a rifle. After gazing a few minutes at the boat, they rode back out of the timber, and took a course parallel with the river, which soon brought them to a point on the bank beyond the cottonwood belt, and close to the steamboat channel. They called several times to those on board, but no one understood their tongue. After a few moments' consultation, they seemed to decide on a new line of action. The two who seemed to be the best mounted, transferred their few articles of camping gear to the other two. and then rode ahead. At a distance of half a mile a herd of about fifty buffalo were quietly feeding, and toward these the two Indians made their way. One was mounted on a handsome white horse, the other on a bay, and both

animals evidently understood the business on which
they were going.  They proceeded at an easy canter
through the sage brush till they reached clear ground
about three hundred yards from the herd.  Here they
diverged, one approaching the animals in flank, the
other from the rear.  At this juncture the approach
of the Indians was discovered, and instantly the herd
was in motion.  Crowding quickly into a compact mass,
they set off at an astonishing pace.  This was the
signal for the hunters.  A loose rein is all the im-
patient horses need, and like an arrow from the
bow, or eagle darting on its prey, they swoop down on
the retreating herd.  Gaining at every stride, they are
soon upon the flanks of the struggling mass.  A puff
of smoke is seen, followed by the sharp crack of a
rifle, but no victim falls.  A few rods farther on, the
bay horse stumbles on uneven ground, and away go
horse and rider rolling on the plain.  But the hunter
is up and remounted almost in an instant, and there
is no pause in the chase.  Clouds of dust rise from the
trampling hoofs, amid which the white horse, like the
famous plume in the helmet of Navarre, can be seen
glancing in the thickest of the fray.  Now the herd
plunges down into a deep coulee, and struggling up
the farther bank continue their flight.  Here the chase
ends.  The hunters dismount and seat themselves on
the river bank, awaiting the approach of the steamer.
In the meantime the other two Indians ride up, and
as we approach one of them lifts up a small kettle, and
puts his hand to his mouth, which we at once inter-

## IV.

### FORT BENTON TO FORT McLEOD

E reached Fort Benton, on the Upper Missouri, on Saturday afternoon, June 10th, in the midst of a pouring rain. We were anxious to camp the same evening, if possible, so as to avoid hotel bills; and we were gratified to find that Mr. David McDougall was still in camp some two miles out of town, having sent on his train of goods, and remained to meet his brother and party. He kindly brought down two teams, and the most necessary articles belonging to the party were taken out. By hard work, tents were pitched and matters got into shape by 10 p.m., and although it rained at intervals during the night, the tents did good service, and we slept in comparative comfort. Some supplies were hurriedly obtained on Saturday evening, and next morning a breakfast of fresh beef, bread and butter and tea, was eaten with a relish. Worship followed, and the remainder of the forenoon was spent in rest. At 3 p.m. we assembled again for worship, when Bro. McLean discoursed profitably from the story of Naaman the Syrian. So passed our first Sabbath under canvas—a day of rest and spiritual refreshment.

We are encamped on the north bank of the Missouri, on a level plateau, some 200 feet above the river. Beneath the lofty banks are beautiful level bottoms, where herds of horses and cattle are grazing. On the south side of the river are the Highwood Hills, which in any other region would pass for lofty mountains. The nearest point, we are informed, is twenty-four miles distant, but in this transparent atmosphere it is difficult to realize that these hills can be more than three or four miles away. On the northern slope of one of the highest peaks patches of snow are distinctly visible.

Benton has about 700 permanent inhabitants; but there is a considerable floating population of ranchmen, freighters, traders, gamblers, &c. Being at present the head of navigation on the Missouri, it is the centre of a vast trade, and is the great distributing point for goods through the western part of the territory, and into our own North-west. There are houses here that handle as much goods, and probably a good deal more money, than the largest wholesale house in Toronto. There is an abundant supply of saloons, restaurants, gambling-houses, and places of still worse repute. Passing along the principal street, I saw immediately inside the open door of a saloon, a table on which lay packs of cards and piles of silver, while

around it sat eight or ten men, busily pursuing their
nefarious business. I did not visit the town on Sunday; but I am told that little difference is made between that and any other day. Boats load and un-
load, shops and gambling-houses are open, and everything goes on as on week days, only " a little more so."
The principal business firm here is that of I. G. Baker
& Co., who in addition to their ordinary trade, have
at present a large and lucrative contract for furnishing
supplies to our Mounted Police in the North-west.
The head of the firm, having made his "pile," does
not now reside here, and the business is managed by
several brothers named Conrad, who have each, I believe, a good paying interest in the concern. In conversation, the elder brother—who has visited Ottawa
and other cities in connection with police contracts—
said he had been struck with the large proportion
of elderly men conducting business in Canada. It
seemed to him that the bank managers and heads of
business houses were almost invariably men of
whitened hair and venerable aspect. "At first," he
said, "they seemed to consider me too young to do
business. I think, however, that you Canadians retain
your health and vigor longer than we Americans.
By the way," he cheerfully continued, "*you* look
remarkably hearty—*for an old man!*"

From Monday to Wednesday was spent in getting
ready for our onward journey, and this left us no spare
moments. Waggons had to be unpacked and put together, horses purchased, supplies provided, not only

3

for the journey, but, in the case of those who were
going to live in the country, to last for six months or
more. By 4 p.m. on Wednesday the work was com--
pleted. Tents were struck, waggons packed, passengers on board, drivers in their places, and then, in remembrance of the mercy that had guided us thus far
we sang—

"Praise God from whom all blessings flow ; "

and turning our faces northward, began the most
serious part of our journey toward the Great Lone
Land. David McDougall led the way with a four
horse waggon, loaded with goods. Eleven other teams
followed, while a number of spare horses were in
charge of George McDougall, jun., to be ready in case
of emergency. With so many animals, some unaccustomed to their work, and nearly all unaccustomed to
their drivers, it is not surprising that a few little
*contretemps* occurred. Occasionally a horse would balk,
while in other cases a pair who pulled hard enough
had a strange objection to pulling at the same time or
in the same direction. Patience and perseverance,
however, overcame these little difficulties, and eventually all settled steadily down to their work.

Some four or five miles from camp we forded the
Teton River, and about eight miles farther descended
a steep hill, and on the banks of the same stream
formed our first night encampment. The waggons
were arranged so as to form a circular enclosure, or
" corrall," into which the horses could be driven when

wanted. A number of these were "hobbled;" a stout rope some thirty feet long, was attached to the neck of each, and allowed to trail on the ground, and then they were turned loose to graze on the prairie till the following morning. Grass is the only food of the native horses during these long and fatiguing journeys, and it seems to meet all their needs.

On Thursday we broke camp at 3 a.m., and after breakfast made a detour to avoid a bad slough, which increased the distance to be travelled by some five or six miles. Our road still led parallel with the Teton River, and on a bend of that stream we rested for dinner. While attending to the horses, &c., a young Indian suddenly made his appearance on horseback among us. He might have dropped from the moon, so silently and unobserved did he appear. A plentiful dinner was given him, which he ate silently, but with evident relish. When he had finished, he disappeared as silently and suddenly as he came. He did not "fold his tent like the Arabs," for he had none; but he "as silently stole away," perhaps to cherish a kindly remembrance of the white strangers who shared their meal with him on the banks of the Teton.

The soil through this part of Montana seems exceedingly poor; still the pasturage must be good, as vast herds of buffalo once roamed these plains. There is an entire absence of timber, and the appearance of the country would indicate that the rainfall is but scant. The soil is hard and dry, and impregnated

with alkali, and this affects the water in the rivers, as
we soon found to our cost,  For several days the heat
has been most intense.  The sun glares down upon
us from a cloudless sky.  Far as eye can reach there
is no shade of bush or tree, and it seems at times as
if we would absolutely faint away.  The heat increases our thirst, which the alkali water does not
allay.  The fine dust penetrates everywhere ; the lips
parch and crack, and mouth and throat become as dry
and sapless as a superannuated sermon.  Heat and
water together destroy appetite and impair digestion,
and it becomes difficult to eat what is necessary to
keep up a moderate degree of strength.  During two
days my rations consisted of three Boston crackers,
and for several days more but a small amount was
eaten.

On Thursday evening we came to a cabin, beside
which we found a well, with an old-fashioned wind-
lass and bucket.  The water was cool and refreshing,
though still tainted with alkali.  A mile or two farther on we camped for the night.

On Friday morning an early start was made, and in
the afternoon we rested at Pend d'Oreille Springs ;
but the water was poor and the heat intense, and it
was decided to journey on through the cool of the
evening.  We started about 5 p.m., and continued on
through the night.  Hour after hour passed, but no
halt.  At length we began to descend by a way so
long and steep that it seemed to be leading to bottom-
less regions ;  and eventually, when the morning star

was above the horizon, the party, thoroughly wearied, reached the banks of the Marias River.

Next morning preparations were made for crossing. On this river there is a scow and rope ferry, by means of which a passage was effected with considerable ease. In the cabin of the man who manages the ferry there is a store, containing supplies of various kinds; and here we found an unlooked-for luxury—a pail of iced water. Dined on the north side of the river, and drove on, amid unabated heat, to 18-mile Coulée. It was thought we might spend the Sabbath at this point; but on reaching it we found insufficient water even for the horses; and therefore it was imperatively necessary to drive on, though the way to the next stopping point was long. About midnight we crossed an alkali plain, where one or two of the more heavily loaded waggons stuck fast, and caused considerable delay before they were extricated. Again the monotonous journey was resumed; fatigue increased to utter weariness; drivers nodded and fell asleep on their waggons, in one case nearly causing a serious runaway; but at last, as dawn was brightening into day, we camped at Rocky Springs for our Sabbath rest. Horses were turned loose, tents were pitched, and the tired travellers got to sleep as quickly as possible. Afterwards, when surveying the ground, we were not sorry we had come so far. Three separate springs issued from openings in the hillside, and joining their waters a rod or two below, went leaping down the slope, clear, bright, and sparkling; while in the adjacent valleys good pasturage was found for the horses. In the afterpart of the day a season of united worship refreshed the spiritual man, and a night's sleep prepared for the toils of the morrow.

On Monday morning a good start was made, and at noon we halted for dinner on the banks of a small stream called Red River, which does not appear on the maps. We were informed that we were now very near the boundary line between the United States and Canada, and early in the afternoon we saw on a hill top one of the conical heaps of stones raised by the Boundary Commission to mark the line. From this point onward there was a marked improvement in the soil, pasturage, and water. The change could not be attributed to imagination, as it was noticed by all the party. About 4 p.m. we crossed Milk River, a beautiful stream, with rich pasturage on either bank, and rested for tea; after which we drove several miles farther, and camped for the night near a small grassy lake. At several points we had evidence that there were mosquitoes and other insect plagues in the land, but here the affliction became serious. "Bull-dog" flies had greatly annoyed the horses during the day, and, as the shadows of evening fell, their place was supplied by clouds of mosquitoes, so that it was next to impossible for our tormented animals to eat a mouthful. To obtain rest for ourselves, a "smudge" fire was kindled in the tent, and the curtain closed. When it was supposed the intruders were sufficiently "sickened," the curtains were opened, and smoke and mosquitoes allowed to escape together. Again the curtains were closed, and with a lighted candle we proceeded to "singe" any straggler left behind. But it seems we did not close our tent with sufficient care, for in the morning we found hundreds of the plagues sticking to the canvas walls. I have speculated much on the possible use of mosquitoes in the economy of nature, but give up the conundrum as too deep for me. I cannot tell what mosquitoes were made for, nor have I found any one who can. Of one thing I am satisfied : Darwin's theory of the " survival of the fittest " is, as applied to mosquitoes, a transparent fraud !

On Tuesday our first halt was at Kipp's Coulée, and our second at 15-mile Butte. After tea we made a detour eastward, to avoid crossing several streams in succession, and about 11 p.m. reached Belly River, below its confluence with the St. Mary's and Old Man's Rivers, and camped for the night. We found the river high, and that it would be impossible to ford it; but a man named Sherin, who has opened a coal mine a short distance down the river, had a couple of flat-bottomed boats, and arrangements were made with him to ferry the party and their goods to the other side. This was no small task. All the waggons had to be unloaded, and their contents transferred piece-meal to the boats. Trunks and boxes were piled in the bottom, to serve as ballast, and then a waggon with two wheels taken off, was nicely balanced on the top. With this ticklish load, in some cases weighing twelve or fifteen hundred pounds, the boat was rowed across

a swift and powerful current to the other side.  Nearly the whole day was consumed in crossing and re-
loading the waggons; but time was precious, and we
drove some ten miles before we camped for the night
on the north bank of the stream.  Near the point
where we crossed, a seam of soft coal, some five feet
thick, and of fair quality, crops out on the bank of
the river.  Considerable quantities are now sent to
Benton and McLeod, and find ready sale.  From this
point northward there is scarcely a stream where coal
may not be found cropping out on the banks.

On Thursday we took dinner on the banks of Old
Man's River, and on resuming our journey the Mc-
Dougalls, Mr. Warren, and myself turned westward to
accompany the Rev. John McLean and wife to Fort
McLeod, while the rest of the party kept on northward.  A pair of fresh horses were put to my waggon,
that we might make better time—an arrangement that
nearly caused a serious accident.  As we neared Mc-
Leod, we found many Indians encamped, as this was
the time for receiving the treaty payments.  On one
side of the road was a thick copse of brushwood, and
on the other the perpendicular bank of Old Man's
River, with a deep and powerful current beneath.
Several children running out from an Indian lodge
close by, frightened the horses, and with a mighty
bound they sprang toward the river.  A second bound
would have taken them over, but David McDougall's
strong arm, by the blessing of God, checked their
course, when they instantly wheeled the other way,

sprang down a bank three feet high, and darted at full speed into the brush. For a few moments things were pretty lively ; but providentially no trees were in the way, and the brushwood, though tall, bent before us without breaking anything, and presently our frightened steeds came to a standstill with nobody hurt.

McLeod is situated at the confluence of Willow Creek and Old Man's River, the latter a powerful stream with a rapid current. There is an unlimited amount of excellent water and good pasturage ; but in other respects the site did not strike me as being well chosen for a military post. It lies low by the river's bank, and commands no view whatever of the surrounding country. In this respect it is in marked, contrast with most of the American posts that we saw which were generally placed so as to command an extensive outlook. As we were now on the north side of Old Man's River, and McLeod is on the south, we had to be ferried over in a boat, a task that occupied less than three minutes, and for which we paid the modest sum of fifty cents apiece each way. One wonders why, with a large police force doing little or nothing, a bridge has not been built, or a rope ferry constructed ; but echo only answers, Why ? *

Bro. and Sister McLean, and the rest of us, were kindly welcomed and hospitably entertained by Mr. J. Smith and his estimable wife. They are from Lower

* I have since been informed that a rope ferry was constructed, but washed away by a freshet, and has not been replaced.

Canada, and Mr. S. is at presant employed in the store of I. G: Baker & Co. Their kind welcome made the missionary and his wife feel at home at once. We visited the parsonage, a hewed log building, but snug and comfortable for a new place. Near by it is a building erected for a school-house, in which worship is conducted. These buildings, I may remark, were secured entirely by local efforts, without any grant from the Society, and reflect great credit on the zeal and enterprise of those who had charge of the work. In 1874 McLeod was established as a post of the Mounted Police. It was afterwards visited at intervals, and service held, by the Rev. John McDougall. Early in 1878 a school was established, and was conducted with great efficiency by Miss Barrett, who had formerly been our teacher at Whitefish Lake. The teacher's salary was met from local sources, and formed no charge upon the Society. In the summer of 1878, Bro. Manning went to McLeod, which thenceforth appeared upon our list of regular missions.

What the future of McLeod may be it is impossible to predict. When the country is opened for settlement, I have no doubt a considerable population will find their way to the fertile bottoms and rich grazing lands of Old Man's River, in which case McLeod may become an important circuit; but I am convinced it cannot be the permanent headquarters of an *Indian* Mission. Indian Missions, to be successful, must be on Indian Reserves, and as far as possible from contact with a white population. There are two points here

which we must occupy at no distant date—the Blood
Reservation, some 15 milesup the river from McLeod ;*
and the Blackfoot Reservation, on Bow River, some
sixty miles below Calgary. In the course of time
other reservations will be set apart for the Piegans and
Sarcees, but the two above mentioned are already located. In the meantime, McLeod is a good point from
which to do preliminary work, as many Indians are
almost constantly to be found around the post ; but as
soon as they begin to settle on their Reserves, the missionary must locate himself among them. The Blackfoot Nation comprises the Blackfeet proper, the Bloods,
Piegans, and Sarcees, all speaking dialects of the same
tongue, and readily understanding one another.

In the evening we prepared to bid good-bye to
Fort McLeod. Bro. and Sister McLean accompanied
us to the landing place, and watched us as we crossed
the stream. Those who travel together over these
uninhabited plains, sharing mutual toils and dangers,
form strong friendships, and there was a feeling of
deep sadness in my heart at this first break in our
party. I could not but think of the isolation, the
discouragements, the trials in store for those we were
leaving to grapple single-handed with the darkness and
ignorance and immorality of surrounding heathenism ;
and as I saw Bro. McLean cheerfully and manfully
bracing himself for his arduous work, and when my
eye rested upon the slight, girlish figure by his side,

---

* This is now occupied by Bro. McLean.

so lately severed from friends and home, and I saw the quivering of her lip, although the brave heart was choking back the tears, I confess my own eyes grew dim, and I said within myself, Thank God, the stuff of which Missionary heroes are made is still to be found in the Church; the heroic age of Methodism is not entirely a thing of the past.

A few strokes of the oars carried us to the north bank of Old Man's River, where, waving a last adieu to the friends on the other side, we resumed our journey, and after a drive of some twelve miles, almost feeling our way through the darkness, we rejoined the rest of the party in their camp on Willow Creek.

# V.

## FORT McLEOD TO MORLEY.

N Friday our first stage took us to the "leav-ings" of Willow Creek, and our second to Pine Coulée. After tea J. McDougall and I took saddle-horses and rode down the coulée and over the hills, while the rest of the party went on by the regular trail. This gave me a better idea of the country off from the immediate line of travel than I could otherwise obtain, though at this particular time the extent of divergence from the road was but small. As we reached the crest of a hill we came upon three splendid horses, evidently of Canadian or American breed, which had strayed from some police camp or Government post. We drove them on before us to where the rest of the party had camped on Mosquito Creek, intending to take them on next day to Calgary ; but the ungrateful brutes left us during the night, and by morning were off, no one knew where. Mosquito Creek was hardly true to its name, as we had less trouble there from the insect plagues than at some other points in our journey.

On Saturday our first stage took us to High River, where we halted for dinner. While the meal was preparing, two Sarcee Indians rode up and dismounted. When they found that McDougall was in the camp they expressed lively satisfaction. On inquiry, I found that McD. had met one of them before under peculiar circumstances, which he related substantially as follows:

"A year or so after going to Morley, a small band of cattle, belonging to a man named Spencer, stampeded in a storm, taking our cows with them. Next day several parties went out in search of them, but could find no trace. Finally I started with two Cree boys to try and find the lost animals. We had ridden hard a good part of the day, and had ascended a small hill for a better outlook, when suddenly we saw two Indians on an opposite hill. They saw us at the same moment, and began riding rapidly back and forth, which we knew was a signal to their friends. Then they galloped some distance toward us, but halted on the opposite side of a narrow valley. I made signs to them to come on, and after some hesitation they did so, singing a war song to stimulate their courage. As they came nearer a swell on the prairie hid them from view, but I could hear the clatter of their horses' hoofs in rapid gallop. A few moments more and they dashed up the hill where we stood, painted and feathered, and each with a revolver at full cock in his hand. I knew but a few words of Blackfoot at the time, and so had to help it out with signs.

When they got close, however, one of the young men recognized me: ' Ah-he-yah ! John ! ' he cried ; ' Ne che-kuh-wow '—' Ah, John ! my friend '—and immediately they jumped from their horses and shook hands cordially. By this time the whole camp were galloping towards us, fully armed. My new friend was very anxious that no harm should befall us, so he rode out and called to the approaching warriors : ' Ke che-kuh-waw na-wuk ; o-o me John,'—' These are our friends ; that is John.' At once the warriors leaped from their horses, and most of them shook hands heartily. A few, however, refused to do so, and sat down with their guns at full cock. I told them what we were doing, and asked if they had seen our cattle. They said No ; they had not tracked any. We continued to talk for some time. I had a breech-loading rifle, which my Indian friend was anxious to get, offering me his horse in exchange. I slipped out the cartridge, and handed him the gun to look at, whereupon an old Indian gave me a quick, warning look, as if to caution me against letting the weapon out of my hands. I told the young Indian I was too far from home to let him have my gun, but if he would come to the Mission I would let him have it. At the same time I had a large-sized Smith & Wesson revolver on a belt beneath my coat. I then said I must be going, as my camp was far. They asked if there was any one in my camp who would trade for robes. I said my brother was there, and if they would send over some of their young men they could probably get what they wanted.

I then mounted with my two Cree boys, and started, being anxious to get out of their way. We rode off at a moderate pace, not knowing what moment a shower of bullets might be sent after us; but as soon as a swell of the prairie hid us from their view, we went off at the gallop. After riding a number of miles, we stopped to make some tea. We had just finished our hasty meal, when three of the young Indians rode up with robes and horses for trade. On we went again at a pace that led one of the Indians to say: 'My brother, you must have very strong medicine; I wish I had some like it.' By-and-by we reached the camp, where my brother traded with them. I saw my Sarcee friend again near the Blackfoot Crossing in 1874, and at the making of the treaty in 1877, and this is why he recognized me so quickly to-day."

After dinner the McDougalls mounted and rode down the stream to look for a crossing. They soon returned, reporting a practicable ford, but hastened our movements by the remark, "You must be quick; the river is rising." Of course, after that, not a moment was lost, and we were soon in motion toward the ford. High River is a large stream, with a strong current, while the "riley" state of the water prevents us from forming any idea of its probable depth. We drive down a steep bank, through some brushwood, and find ourselves at the water's edge. There is no time to hesitate. In we go, McDougall on horseback showing the way. The water proved to be not more than three feet deep, but the strong current dashed it

against waggons and horses with a force that seemed
sufficient to sweep them all away. However, no
accident happened, and soon all were safely over. But
now we found we had crossed only one branch of the
river, and that another and a deeper one was yet to be
got over. David McDougall's carts had crossed the
first branch just before us, and we passed them in
the brush as we drove towards the second crossing.
Reaching the bank, we found the stream narrower
than the former, but the bank was exceedingly steep,
and the deepest water was immediately beneath it. It
seemed as though the waggon must inevitably pitch
over on the horses' backs; but we must venture.
Down the bank we go, and plunge into the river. The
angry current retorts by a dash that sends the water
over the waggon box; but almost before one has time
to regain his breath, our sturdy little ponies have
struggled through, and are safe on the other side.
The other waggons followed, and all eventually got
across. I may mention that one team was driven
throughout the journey by Mrs. Sibbald, wife of our
teacher at Morley, and another by her son, a lad about
fourteen. Their pluck and self-reliance were worthy
of all admiration. As soon as our party were safely
over, the carts began crossing, and accomplished the
task safely; but while some other carts were following,
a few minutes later, one of them upset, sending eight
sacks of flour into the river. These were subsequently
recovered, not much damaged.

We rested on the bank of the river for tea, and
4

at 7 p.m. were again on the way. J. McDougall led and I followed, outstripping the rest of the teams. Before dark we reached Sheep Creek, which we found to be a rushing river. Without waiting to take soundings, we plunged in, and by a very circuitous ford got safely to the other side, and driving on a little farther camped on a beautiful bottom for our Sabbath rest. The remainder of the party soon joined us, glad of a chance to rest awhile. The only drawback to our comfort was the cloud of mosquitoes that came down upon us like the locusts of Egypt. We "smudged" them to the best of our ability, but they nearly drove the horses wild.

At this point a few words about the country through which we have passed may not be out of place. I have previously said that we noticed an improvement in the soil and vegetation after crossing the boundary line, and this became more marked as we proceeded. Milk River, but a few miles north of the boundary, offers excellent facilities for stock raising, and, I should judge, for agriculture also. The grass is rich, vetches are abundant, and the soil thrown up by the badgers seems of excellent quality. Through all this region there is an entire absence of timber; but coal crops out on most of the rivers, which settles the question of fuel, and timber in considerable quantities can be found among the foothills and in the mountains. Whether the ridges and uplands will be found suitable for farming purposes can be settled only by experiment, but we had ocular demonstration that they furnish pasturage of the best quality, while on the line of the rivers, at least, there is abundance of excellent water. We were told we should find the land getting still better, and the water better and more abundant, as we got further north— a statement which we fully verified. Sheep Creek, where we were now camped, struck me as a choice location. The water is good and plentiful, the soil on the bottoms a rich black loam of great depth, and there is a limited supply of timber—spruce and poplar—along the stream, enough for building and fencing. I am convinced that, in this locality both farming and stock-raising might be profitably pursued.

On Monday morning we left Sheep Creek. For some time our way was "onward and upward" over the richest soil and vegetation we had yet seen. Grass and vetches were fresh and rank, the soil rich and black, and where thrown up by the moles and badgers was as fine and mellow as the soil of a thoroughly worked garden. It must not be understood that the soil throughout the whole country is of this character. Many of the hills and uplands are gravelly or stony but even there the pasturage is excellent, and there is on the whole very much less waste land than in almost any part of the older provinces that I have yet visited.

Proceeding on our way, a little before noon we suddenly came in sight of evidences of civilization. Some distance before us we saw a very neat house of hewed logs, with outbuildings and well fenced fields. Near the house ran the waters of Fish Creek,

with a growth of poplar on either bank. We were
told that this was "Glenn's Ranch," and as we reached
it the proprietor himself came out and gave us friendly
greeting. Mr. Glenn is an Irishman, who came from
British Columbia and settled on Fish Creek in 1875,
and is the person of that name to whom Principal
Grant refers in his book, "From Ocean to Ocean."
He has about eighteen acres under cultivation, with
every prospect of an abundant harvest. He told me
that last year from one acre and three quarters of
barley he threshed 6,000 pounds, or over 71 bushels
(American standard) to the acre. From four and a
half acres of oats he took 9,000 pounds, or over 57
bushels to the acre, and half of this was from the
"sod," *i.e.,* the first year of ploughing, when only
about one-third of an average crop is expected. On
Mr. Glenn's table we found the *Weekly Globe,* showing
that he has by no means lost his interest in the outside
world. He seemed to have but one objection to the
country. Said he, "We have no protection from the
police. The Indians may steal our cattle, as they often
do, but we can get no redress. In that respect we
would be better off if there were no police in the
country at all."

After dinner, to which a generous bunch of onions
from Mr. Glenn's garden gave additional zest, we
were favored by a call from Mr. Wright—brother of
Dr. George Wright, of Toronto—the gentlemanly
superintendent of the Government Supply Farm,
situated about two miles further down Fish Creek. I

may explain that while instructors are sent to teach
the Indians how to cultivate the soil, there are " Supply
Farms," apart from the Reserves, used for the purpose
of raising food and seed grain for the Indians. This
strikes me as a wise arrangement. The buffalo having
disappeared from the country, the Indians will probably
have to be fed at intervals for years to come, and
supplies can be raised more cheaply in the country
than they can be imported. A few of us accompanied
Mr. Wright on a visit to the farm. It lies at the
confluence of Fish Creek and Bow River, and comprises some 5,000 acres of splendid bottoms and
rolling prairie. Nearly 200 acres are now under
cultivation, embracing seven acres of potatoes, eight
of turnips, 100 of wheat, the rest oats and barley.
Mr. Wright expects to have 500 acres broken up and
under cultivation next year ; but he labors under the
disadvantage of unsuitable and insufficient farm
machinery. If the Government intends to make
these farms a success, it will pay well to supply the
superintendents with the best appliances for carrying
on their work. Mr. Wright's house is of hewed logs,
well built, containing but moderate comforts and no
luxuries. Bidding the courteous superintendent good-
bye, we drove rapidly toward Calgary, in the teeth of
a very cold wind, and at dusk rejoined our party on
the banks of Bow River.

Next morning we awoke to the fact that there was
" one more river to cross," for immediately at our feet
rolled the waters of the Bow, a stream some 250 or 300

yards wide, and with a volume and current strong enough, apparently, to run all the machinery in Ontario. Of course there was no bridge, and fording was out of the question. Only a few days later, a policeman, attempting to ford higher up, was drowned, together with five horses. But D. McDougall had secured a boat at Fort Calgary, and had it in readiness to ferry over goods, waggons, and passengers. Again we had to pass through an experience similar to that at Belly River. Goods had to be unpacked and transferred to the boat ; waggon wheels taken off, so as to get the vehicles on board ; but by dint of hard labor, goods, waggons, and passengers were safely over by about 3 p.m. Not feeling equal to a full share of the labor which others had to perform, I mounted a horse and rode to Calgary, a Hudson Bay post a mile up the river, to see if I could obtain some assistance. Seeing a man in front of a house, I asked him if he knew where I could get a man to help in ferrying some goods and waggons across the river. "Well," he said, "there are no men here just now ; they are all away at the treaty payments ; but I don't mind if I go down and give you a lift myself." On inquiry, I found the name of this "friend in need" was Joe Butler, that he hailed from Kingston, Ont., had been connected in some way with the Mounted Police, and was now managing a ranch for an officer of the force. He worked with a will until all our party were safely over, but refused to receive any compensation. " No," said he ; " we calculate to help one another in this country, and perhaps I may want some help myself some day." The Lord bless kind-hearted Joe Butler!

After getting goods, vehicles, and passengers safely over, the horses were still to be got across. They were driven into the stream, and though some appeared loth to try the current, they all eventually struck out. Most of them landed on the point of an island about three-fourths of the way over, where they rested awhile, and then of their own accord entered the narrower channel and quickly swam accross. A few of the weaker ones were carried further down the stream, and it seemed as though one or two would be lost; but strong hands were on the shore, and by means of a strong rope the struggling animals were helped up the steep bank to a place of safety. While watching the horses as they swam over, my attention was especially drawn to one of the mules. Now a horse, when swimming, gets more or less excited. He puts his muscle into the work, and keeps up a vigorous snorting during the whole passage. But a mule—or at least this particular mule—did none of these things. She entered the stream deliberately, neither slackening nor quickening her usual gait. The deepening of the current did not change her aspect of profound melancholy. When she could no longer touch bottom, she floated away with the stoical indifference of an orthodox Mussulman. Not a snort, not a plunge, not a struggle; but with an expression of hopeless indifference, as of one who has so long borne

" The stings and arrows of outrageous fortune "

that he has no longer anything to hope or fear, the
solemn beast went calmly floating down. It seemed
as if an earthquake, or the discharge of a whole park
of artilery, would not have caused the slightest stait,
or a single wag of those majestic ears. Of all sights
combining the indescribably solemn with the indescribably ludicrous, I have seen nothing to equal the
spectacle of that ancient mule floating down the
current of Bow River. It may satisfy the reader to
know that she got safely over, and completed the rest
of the journey without accident.

About a mile above where we crossed, and on the
south side of the river, is Fort Calgary, a post of the
Hudson Bay Company. A little above this, Elbow
River forms a junction with the Bow ; and in the angle
between the two is situated a post of the Mounted
Police, sometimes called Calgary, but more frequently
the " Elbow." At this point there is a small church,
erected by John McDougall, who, with the assistance
of the teacher at Morley, got out the timber near the
mountains and rafted it down Bow River, a distance
of over sixty miles. ·The building was erected without cost to the Society·

After crossing Bow River we rested a little, and
refreshed ourselves with a cup of tea, after which we
resumed our journey. A few miles out the party
separated, Messrs. Glass and Youmans taking the
direct road north to Edmonton, while the rest of the
party turned west toward Morley. That night we
camped at Rolling Hills, some ten miles from Calgary.

During the forenoon of the following day, we came
near having a serious accident. J. McDougall was
leading the way with a waggon containing his mother,
wife, and two children; next came his daughter Flora
and Miss Adams in a buckboard, and my own conveyance followed. Bro. McD. had halted to arrange
some luggage that was not securely tied, and I had
driven a few steps off the road, when we heard a great
commotion behind us. Looking round, we saw a pair
of harnessed horses dashing toward us at full speed,
and all the spare horses stampeding in the same
direction. At first they were taking a course parallel
to the road, a short distance from it; but when within
a few paces of the standing waggons they suddenly
wheeled into the road and dashed straight at the
buckboard. On reaching it they partially divided, one
of the animals striking the vehicle a tremendous blow
on one of the wheels, bending the axle, and throwing
the whole forward, on the other horses. These,
terrified in their turn, wheeled and darted off, jerking
the lines out of Miss McDougall's hands, and throwing
her to the ground, one of the wheels going over her
body, but without doing her any serious injury, while
Miss Adams still retained her seat. Meanwhile the
horses who first ran away, still more terrified by the
collision, bounded forward and the next moment struck
the waggon containing Mr. McDougall's family, over-
turning it in an instant. The horses attached to this
vehicle being now, in turn, thoroughly terrified, gave
a tremendous bound, snapped one whippletree in two,

and broke the irons of the other, and joined the
general stampede. All this passed in, perhaps, twenty
seconds. A glance showed Bro. McDougall that his
family, by almost a miracle, had escaped unhurt, and
instantly he sprang round a clump of bushes to try to
intercept the horses who were running away with the
buckboard; but finding this impossible, he called to
Miss Adams to throw herself out. She had still
presence of mind enough to understand and obey his
instructions, and alighting on the soft, thick grass,
escaped entirely unhurt. All this, as I have said
passed in a few seconds, and when it was over we
could only stand for a time in speechless thankfulness
to God that no lives had been lost. Mr. McDougall's
buckboard was badly injured, and had to be left
by the wayside, and his other waggon was slightly
damaged, and that was all. In the meantime the
runaway animals were overtaken and brought back
by the horsemen, after a run of several miles. On
inquiry we learned that the cause of the accident was
the breaking of a chain, by which the leaders of
D. McDougall's four-horse team had got away.

Passing over some very rich uplands and rolling
prairie, we descended a succession of hills, and about
noon reached the banks of Big Hill Creek, where we
rested for dinner. This creek we found contained
abundance of fine trout, a number of which were
caught in a few minutes and prepared for use.
Shortly after, the first rain-storm we had encountered
since leaving Benton broke sudddnly upon us, and for

a time torrents of rain, mingled with hail, descended;
but in the course of an hour the sky cleared, and we
were again in motion. About 6 p.m. we reached the
high bank of Ghost River, a few yards above its
junction with the Bow. We had heard a good deal
about this stream, and Mrs. McDougall had tersely
described it by saying: "Ghost River is not very
large, but it's wicked. When the water is high, I
consider it one of the most dangerous streams in the
country." In fact this "ghost" had haunted us for
several days, and now we actually had a sight of it·
Nor was the sight very reassuring. The stream was
swift, the depth unknown, and just below where we
must attempt to ford there was a strong rapid, and
just below this again the rolling waters of Bow River.
Bro. McDougall mounted a horse and proceeded to try
the ford. He soon came back and said he thought we
could cross all right. But first the waggons must
be got down the worst hill we had yet encountered.
By careful work this was safely accomplished. Then
one by one, the waggons ventured in, and eventually
all got over, although in one or two cases a stout rope,
manned by willing hands, was a great assistance. As
for myself, I preferred a saddle-horse to the chances of
an upset from a waggon, and the sagacious animal that
I mounted went through the stream as though he was
quite used to that kind of business, as indeed I
suppose he was. At all events the "ghost" was laid
for that time, and we were told that we were within
six miles of Morley. Some time had been consumed

in crossing the river, and it was dark when we resumed our way ; but stimulated by the prospect of approaching rest in a Christian home, we travelled cheerily on, and ere long found ourselves welcomed into the unpretentious but comfortable Mission-house at Morley. To be once more in a veritable house, to sit down at a well-spread table, and then, after gratefully acknowledging the goodness that had followed us through all our journeyings, to lie down on a comfortable bed, was all inexpressibly delightful ; but we were too tired for speech, or even for thought, and soon sank into dreamless repose.

## VI.

## AT MORLEY—SABBATH SERVICES.

HE valley of Bow River comprises one of the most beautiful sections of country in the North-West, and offers facilities for stock raising and agriculture that it would be difficult to surpass. The level bottoms are large and the soil of the best; the slopes and hills are covered with abundant pasture, the deep valleys afford excellent shelter, the water is good and plentiful, while the winters, as a rule, are so mild that stock can stay out with perfect safety and come in fat in the spring. To those who contemplate stock raising there is no part of the country I have yet seen which offers so many attractions as the valley of the Bow.

Morley Mission is situated on the river at a point about fifteen miles below where it issues from the mountains. The site and its surroundings are very beautiful. The general course of the river is first east, and then south-east; but a little above Morley it takes a turn northward, sweeping around the

mission premises in a graceful curve. Standing on
the first "bench" above the level bottom, and facing
westward, the first object that strikes one's attention
is the mission-house, a modest structure, built of
hewed logs and weather-boarded; about 48 feet wide
by 22 feet deep, and perhaps 11 or 12 feet high to the
eaves. The interior is divided by partitions of boards,
tongued and grooved, plaster—except clay—being yet
unknown in the country. Behind the mission-house
are the outbuildings, constructed of logs. A little
to the right, and in the same enclosure with the
mission-house, is the cottage of the teacher, built of
hewed logs, "chinked" and plastered with clay. To
the left are the walls of an unfinished building,
intended as the future mission-house, when the present
one may be used for another purpose. A few rods
farther from the river are the church and school-house,
two neat and commodious buildings, well adapted for
their respective purposes. Away to the right, across
a small creek, is the house, store, &c., of Mr. David
McDougall; while on a level plain, back of the church,
stand some 30 Stoney tents, and back of these two
very neat cabins belonging to Indians who have
settled down to farming. Still farther away are the
rolling foothills of the Rocky Mountains, their sides
and summits, in many cases, adorned with groves of
poplar, spruce, and mountain pine, while forming a
grand background to the picture, the mountains themselves tower upward, their scarred and weather-beaten
sides softened by a haze of blue, their summits often

wreathed in cloud and vapor, through the rifts of which masses of yet unmelted snow shine with dazzling whiteness, contrasting beautifully with the neutral tints of the rocks around.

Although Morley is one of the youngest missions in the Saskatchewan District, it is one of the most promising. When Dr. Taylor visited the spot in 1873, the mission was not yet begun ; not even a log had been cut for the projected buildings ; but the McDougalls had explored the ground, and saw that here was the place to reach on the one hand the Stoneys who had heard the Gospel from Rundle and Woolsey in former years, and on the other the Crees and Blackfeet of the plains. Although strongly dissuaded, on account of the perilous nature of the enterprise, in thus placing themselves in the very focus between hostile tribes, they persevered in their design ; and in the fall of 1873, John McDougall and his family, and his brother David, made their way out from Edmonton, and by the shores of a small lake, in a sheltered spot among the hills, about three miles above the present mission, they proceeded to erect a shelter for the winter, and a little church and school-house besides. In the cabin thus erected they lived two years, preparing material meanwhile for permanent buildings on a better site near the river. No one unacquainted with the nature of the work and the surroundings can form the least idea of the labor involved in this latter undertaking. The logs being cut and squared, had to be drawn about three miles,

while every foot of timber used in the construction of
the buildings had to be sawn by hand, there being no
such thing as a saw-mill in any part of the country.
The nearest place to obtain hardware was Fort Benton,
more than 400 miles away, where common nails cost
12 cents a pound, and other things in proportion.
Besides this frequent journeys had to be made to the
plains and elsewhere for supplies of food, involving
altogether thousands of miles of travel, and leaving
the mission family unprotected for weeks together.
But through all these troubles the Missionary and
his family persevered, and mission-house, teacher's
house, church, and school-house were successively
erected, towards which the Society made but one
grant of $900—a mere fraction of what the whole
thing must have cost—while no claim for travelling
expenses was ever made ; and this at a time when
flour—if it could be got at all—was never less than
from twelve to fifteen dollars per sack of 100 lbs., and
other things, except buffalo meat, in the same proportion. Around the mission-house several fields have
been fenced and brought under cultivation ; and
looking for a moment only at material results I confess
I am astonished at the progress made at Morley in so
short a time.

The effect of all this upon the Indians has been
most salutary. It has led them to see how much
better it is to till the soil than to depend for a liveli-
hood upon the uncertainties of the chase. And now
that a considerable tract of land on both sides of the

river has been set apart as the Stoney Reserve; many are settling down, building cabins, and beginning to cultivate their little fields. Last year one of the Government Farm Instructors, a Mr. Gowan, was sent to Morley, and entered heartily upon his work. He showed the Indians how to fence their fields and cultivate the soil, and induced them to work to a degree beyond what had been accomplished in any other place. The Indians, convinced that Mr. Gowan had their interests at heart, were greatly pleased; but unfortunately for himself, he uttered his mind too freely in regard to some doings of the police authorities, and they never rested till he was dismissed. At all events, this is the explanation of Mr. G.'s removal current among the people, and fully believed. The Indians are greatly disappointed and discouraged. Mr. Gowan had gained their confidence in a remarkable degree, and they were prepared to co-operate with him in his further efforts for their advancement. His successor, so far as I can learn, has accomplished nothing, because he has attempted nothing. Hitherto, at least, he has only served out rations (assisted therein by a policeman), and the Indians say he has not yet so much as seen most of their fields. He assigns as the reason for this do-nothing policy, that he is waiting for the arrival of one of the Farm Inspectors to tell him what to do.*

During my stay at Morley I had good opportunity of seeing the agricultural implements furnished by the

* This was written in August, 1880.

5

Government to the Indians. By treaty stipulation
there was to be a plow for every three families. It
was, of course, understood by the Indians that these
would be what are called "breaking plows,"—no other
kind being of any service whatever in breaking up the
prairie. Some idea of the quality of those actually
furnished may be inferred from the fact that although I
am by no means a good specimen of "muscular Christianity," I picked up one of the plows in my hands and
carried it across the yard with the greatest ease. I
next took up a whippletree, which some slight accident
had broken in two, and found it to be a half-rotten
stick, no stronger than a piece of black ash. The
harrows, in weight and strength, were about suitable
for a well-plowed garden. Other implements were
very similar. I surveyed the assortment, and felt in
my "inner consciousness" that

> " For ways that are dark,
> And for tricks that are vain,
> The *Government Contractor* is peculiar,
> Which the same I will always maintain."

Thursday and Friday were given to rest and letter-
writing, varied by a visit to the school conducted by
Mr. Sibbald. The attendance a few days before had
been over 40, but at the time of my visit it was less
than 20. The annuities having been recently paid,
the parents were busy making purchases at the store,
and the temptation to see what was bought was too
strong for most of the children. Some of the scholars
present could read in the first book with tolerable

METHODIST MISSION PREMISES, MORLEY.

readiness, and the smaller ones could read the alphabet backwards or forwards, up or down, without a mistake. Hitherto, the migratory habits of the people have been a great drawback to school work. This is especially true of the Stoneys, of whom other Indians say it is a rare thing for a Stoney to camp two nights on the same spot. As the people settle down on their reserves, this difficulty will be overcome. Another spot of no small interest, that received an early visit, was the little graveyard on a hill behind the mission, where we stood for a time with uncovered heads beside the grave of our noble missionary, George McDougall. It is enclosed by a board fence, and a suitable monument has been provided by his children, which only awaits transport from Fort Benton in order to be set up over the grave. They have also provided three tablets to be set up in the three churches he labored so hard to establish—namely, at Morley, Edmonton, and Victoria. There is another spot which I think the whole Church should mark by a suitable monument, of which I will speak in another place.

On Saturday we took saddle horses and set out for a canter over the hills. This ride confirmed my first impressions of the beauty of the country around Morley, and the wisdom of the choice which had located a mission there. We rode past the site of the first buildings, and found some of the cabins in a tolerable state of perservation. Along the hill sides and in the valleys are extensive groves of poplar, spruce, and mountain pine. It must not be supposed, however, that the country is "timbered" in the sense in which we would use that term in Ontario or Quebec, but timber in sufficient quantities for building and fencing can easily be obtained, while a good portable saw-mill could find ample employment, and, I doubt not, a ready market for its lumber, for many a year to come. In the course of our ride we passed a number of small fields which have been enclosed and cultivated by the Indians. Some of these are clean and well kept, and give promise of a good harvest in due time. Several cabins have also been erected, one being two stories high and neatly built. I am persuaded that if these Stoneys receive reasonable instruction and encouragement they will soon be able to provide for their own wants, irrespective of what they may obtain by hunting.

## VII.

### SABBATH SERVICES.

UNDAY was a high day at Morley. The poor Stoneys were delighted at the return of their missionary, and many came to the mission-house the morning after our arrival, to give him greeting. The band to which the reserve has been alloted numbers, I believe, over 600 souls, and a large proportion of these have been near the mission for some time. At half-past 10 service was held in the school-house, the church having been "appropriated," during the Missionary's absence, as a storehouse for agricultural implements, and there being no time to get it in readiness for the Sabbath service. The building was crowded to its utmost capacity, a large proportion of the people seating themselves on the floor in true Indian fashion, while those who sat on the benches by the wall manifested a strong disposition to take a "lower seat" in the synagogue before the service was over. Most of the Indians were but poorly clad, which Bro. McDougall tells me is accounted for solely by the fact of "hard times," the Indians

having experienced difficulty the past year in obtaining
sufficient food by hunting, let alone the wherewithal
to buy clothing. 'The past season has been one of
great destitution, owing to the disappearance of the
buffalo ; and down on the plains cases were not uncommon of individuals, and even of whole families,
starving to death./ In conducting the service Brother
McDougall used the Cree language, which a number
of the people understood. After singing and prayer he
read part of the 3rd of John, and spoke for some
fifteen minutes ; then after another hymn he spoke
again, still in Cree, Chief Jacob Big-Stoney interpreting. Jacob seemed master of the situation, interpreting
rapidly and with very little hesitation. The congregation behaved, in some respects, very much like an
English one. All were quiet, a few nodded and slept,
a few were restless and indifferent, but the greater
portion listened with close attention. The babies, who
were present in considerable numbers, were not as
silent as Indian babies are commonly represented to be,
and some of them cried in remarkably good English.
It would seem as if, when language was confounded
at Babel, laughing and crying were excepted, for there
is no difference in these sounds the wide world over.
I am told, however, that Indian mothers insist that all
babies laugh and cry, not in English but in Indian ;
and I suppose a similar claim would be made by the
natives of every clime and tongue beneath the sun. It
is said a Yorkshireman in France became fairly home-
sick in his longing for the sound of his mother tongue ;

and when, early one morning, he heard the vigorous braying of a donkey, he rapturously exclaimed, "There, thank God, I hear English once more!" But this is a digression.

In the afternoon I crossed the river with Bro. McDougall in a " skin " boat, to hold service in a camp on the South side. Perhaps some one may ask " What is a *skin* boat ?" It is a vessel constructed in this wise : First, a frame is made of willow boughs, the shape being a cross between a skiff and a canoe. Over this is stretched an untanned hide (two if the boat be large), with the flesh side to the water, and securely fastened. And when this dries it becomes as tight as a drum-head, and if well made is a safe and serviceable boat. The one in which we crossed had lain long in the water, and was thoroughly soaked ; but the river was not very wide, and we soon got over. After landing we walked about a mile and a-half, accompanied by several Indians who had crossed with us, which brought us to the camp of Chief Bear's Paw. James Dixon, one of our converted Stoneys, was also there, and by the vigorous use cf a good-sized dinner-bell summoned the people together. There were about thirty tents, and the usual number of dogs and horses. Several fields containing barley, potatoes, &c., were within sight, also several neat cabins that had been erected during the past year. When the people came together, there had to be a general hand-shaking all round, with men, women, and children, before service began. The mothers would even hold out the hands of their little babies so that they might not be overlooked. I had prudently made myself familiar with the Stoney form of salutation—" Ambu wastage !" equivalent to our " Good day,"—and was therefore able to hold my own during the hand-shaking business. The salutations over, the people seated themselves on the ground and service began. A hymn was sung, and Bro. McDougall prayed in Cree. A number of children had been brought for baptism, but before attending to these a number of marriages were celebrated. No less than six couples were thus united. Then came the baptism of twelve children, Scripture names largely predominating. All this occupied a considerable time, after which I was called upon to speak to the people. Bro. McDougall had said to me that as I might not have another opportunity of speaking to this part of the band, a general address, mingling advice on both temporal and spiritual matters, would perhaps be better than a sermon. I accordingly addressed them somewhat in this wise, McDougall translating into Cree and James Dixon into Stoney :—

" My brothers, I have come far to see you. The lodges of my people are very far away towards the rising sun. But I have often heard about you. The Missionary sent messages saying that the Stoneys had listened to the words of the Master of Life. Then our hearts were glad, for we had read in the Book of the Great Spirit that the good news of Jesus Christ was the power of God to save every one who believed it whether he was a white man or a red. And we prayed to the Master of Life that he would bless all the Stoneys, and teach them the way of salvation.

"Last spring a council of some of the praying chiefs of my people was held, and they said to me—'You must go westward; go on the long path over river and plain, and see our brothers who live under the shadows of the great mountains, towards the setting sun. Tell them we are glad because they have received the words of the Master of Life from the mouth of the Missionary. Tell them how the white man and the red man live as brothers here, because they both have received the words of peace from the Great Spirit and his Son Jesus Christ; and speak to them words of counsel, so that the Stoney may know what is best for himself and his children.' So I have come to speak in your ears to-day.

"The Stoneys are wise: their eyes and ears are always open; but it is not the wisdom of the white man. The Stoney knows how to hunt the buffalo on the plains, and follow the deer on the hills; he knows how to track the bear in the mountains, and shoot the wild goat on the rocks; he knows how to trap the beaver on the streams, and catch the fish in the rivers; and his women know how to dress the skin of the deer or the buffalo, and make a warm lodge for the winter. But when deer and buffalo are gone, and there is hunger in his tent, the Stoney does not yet know, like the white man, how to bring food out of the ground, or to build a warm lodge without skin of buffalo or deer.

"Now, let my brothers listen; let them open their eyes and look. Do they hear the tramp of the buffalo on the plains? Can they see the deer bounding over the hills? Can they show me where the beaver builds his lodge by the streams? No! The buffalo are all gone; the deer is hard to find; the beavers are very few. It is plain the Stoney can no longer live as he has done. He must learn to live as does the white man. He must learn to till the soil, and no longer depend upon what he can get by hunting. I am glad to see some of you are trying to do this. I have seen your fields, and the houses you have built, and I have said—The Stoney need be hungry no more; if he goes on as he has begun, he will have plenty for himself and for his children.

"But if the Stoney is to live like the white man, his children must be taught like the children of the white man. It is for this we have established a school among you, and we want you to send your children there to be taught those things which make the white man wise and strong. Above all, we want them to be able to read for themselves the Book of the Great Spirit, for without this all other wisdom will be as nothing.

"I have spoken to you about the things of this life; but there is somthing far more important. Very soon I will return to my people, and you will see my face no more; but before I go I want to speak again the words you have often heard from your Missionary— that Jesus Christ came into the world to save sinners, and that whosoever trusts in Him and obeys His voice shall not perish, but shall have everlasting life. And when in days to come your Missionary may send letters to tell me about you, I hope to hear that you did not forget the words of the white stranger who came into your camp to-day; but that you are all listening to the teachings of the Master of Life, and trusting in His Son Jesus Christ."

Service over, there was another general hand-shaking, and we turned our faces homeward. Several Indians accompanied us; but when we came to the river side we found our boat more than half full of water. An examination of our craft showed two small holes in the bottom through which the water had entered. The Indians were equal to the emergency. One of the men produced a needle; a woman drew out of some hidden receptacle some fibres of the deer's sinew, and in a short space of time the boat was mended, and the passengers ferried safely over the river.

In the evening another service was held in the school-house. I undertook to preach, Bro. McDougall interpreting; but I must confess I have heard many a better sermon. This preaching through an interpreter makes sad work. After service six couples were married and sixteen children presented for baptism. One young fellow hesitated a good deal in regard to the marriage business, but we subsequently learned it was entirely on conscientious grounds; he didn't like to make the promises involved in the marriage vow without feeling sure that he would be able to keep them. However, he finally made the venture. In the baptismal service Bro. McDougall got things mixed a little, owing probably to the large number of candidates. He was about to christen one baby Enoch, but discovered just in time that it wasn't that kind of a baby, and that its parents desired to call it Flora ; so Flora it was baptized. These varied services had well filled up a busy day, and we returned to the mission house somewhat wearied in body, but thankful for the experience of a Sunday at Morley.

## VIII.

## A DAY IN THE MOUNTAINS.

HEN about three days out from Benton, we caught our first glimpse of the Rocky Mountains, then more than a hundred miles away, and from that time we were rarely out of sight of some of the loftier peaks. Each day's journey brought us a little nearer, and when we reached Calgary, the mountains were but forty miles distant. From that point, as previously stated, our course was westward till we reached Morley, when we were within fifteen miles of the stony giants. This nearer view only intensified the desire to penetrate one of the passes, and climb, if possible, some of those rugged steeps. Arrangements were accordingly made for a brief excursion, and before noon on Monday, the 3rd, we were ready for the trail. First a horse was packed with such camping apparatus as was considered indispensable—to wit, some bedding, a tarpaulin or waggon-sheet, an axe, frying-pan, and camp kettle, and last, though not least, a bag of pro-

A ROCKY MOUNTAIN STREAM.

visions. To "pack" a horse properly requires experience. You first lay on the horse's back a well-folded blanket; over this is placed the pack saddle, which exactly resembles a diminutive saw-horse, and the girth or "sinch" is drawn up till you are in momentary expectation of seeing the unfortunate animal part in the middle and become a span. But no such catastrophe occurs, and you proceed to arrange the rest of the load. The various articles are placed so as to balance on either side, and the whole is securely and firmly tied to the pack-saddle and around the horse's body. While this is being done, other horses are saddled for the party, and we mount and away. Riding out through the Stoney camp, Chief Chin-a-kee is invited to come with us as guide, to which he readily agrees. Our ride for the first two or three hours is among the foothills of the Rockies, affording us some beautiful views of the upper valley of the Bow; then we descend a hill as steep as the roof of a house (a Mansard roof at that), and strike the valley of the south branch of Ghost River, which we follow up towards the mountains. During the season of rain or melting snows, Ghost River is a torrent wide, deep, and strong; later in the season the water quickly subsides, and the stream divides into numerous channels, with gravelly islands between. In this state we found it—a fortunate circumstance for us, as we had to ford the various branches not less than twenty times. We halt to lunch and to feed the horses, and at 2 p.m. resume our ride. Chin-a-kee

leads the way, apparently at an easy jog-trot, but
manages to get over the ground at a rate which puts
us on our mettle. Now we canter over a long stretch
of gravel, plunge into one of the numerous channels,
clamber up the opposite bank, off again over an Indian
trail, through groves of spruce and poplar; and this is
repeated again and again for miles together. About
16 miles out from Morley we leave the valley of Ghost
River and turning sharp to the left enter a cañon
about a quarter of a mile wide, with mighty cliffs
towering up on either hand. The timber is thick and
much of it fallen, and the trail at times hardly per-
ceptible. Soon we come to a long stretch where the
timber has recently been destroyed by fire, and we
have to pick our way as best we can among the
charred remains. Passing the burnt portion, we find
the undergrowth thicker than ever, and although the
trail under foot is tolerably distinct, yet how anything
larger than a dog can possibly get through is a profound mystery. But our Kayoose ponies are equal to
the emergency. They creep through brushwood, turn
sharp corners, glide between trees, wade through bogs,
step cannily among roots and boulders, and make
their way safely and quietly where an average Ontario horse would go wild and break his own legs or
his rider's neck in five minutes. One never ceases to
wonder at the sagacity, pluck, and endurance of these
native horses.

Our destination is Long Lake, some ten or twelve
miles up the cañon; but before reaching it we pass

6

several smaller lakes, formed chiefly by the melting
snows of the surrounding mountains. During last
winter the snow-fall was unusually heavy; consequently we find the water in the lakes three or four
feet higher than common, entirely covering and oblit-
erating the trail. We try to surmount this difficulty
by a flank movement, which takes us over acres of
fallen timber and through dense brushwood, where
the only trail is the one we make. In this way, however, we pass two lakes; a third offers more serious
difficulties. The overflow has spread out among the
willows, and fills the cañon, for a short distance, from
side to side. But we started for Long Lake and to
Long Lake we are resolved to go. We push on till the
water becomes threateningly deep, when the leader
prudently retraces his steps to look for a safer way.
The Chief and McDougall lead off to the right, and I
follow. Soon there is considerable splashing and
plunging ahead, but I can see nothing, as the willows
are dense and high. It is literally a case of " follow
your leader," and there is no time to stop and ask
questions; go ahead, and you will see for yourself.
Exactly! The thought has scarcely flashed through
my mind before my pony is up to his withers in snow
water, and my long riding-boots are filled up to the
brim. But who cares! The free mountain air is in
our lungs, the thrill of its inspiration in the blood,
and there seems to be something in the very atmosphere that renders one fearless of danger and careless
of discomfort. So, making merry over our impromptu

cold bath, which all had shared, we passed the water, and jog on again. Now the trail leads along the steep side of a slope formed by the *debris* of centuries from the neighboring cliff. It inclines at an angle of about sixty degrees, and the path is but like a goat track, where a single false step would send horse and rider rolling down the bank to plunge into deep water forty feet below. But our ponies are not in the habit of making false steps. We simply give them a loose rein, and they take us along as quickly and safely as an ordinary horse would do on a level road. About sunset we pass the last of the small lakes, and prepare to camp for the night. Horses are unsaddled, and turned loose to graze, for even in this deep cañon the grass is tolerably abundant. A fire is kindled, and burns cheerfully amid the gathering gloom; supper is cooked and eaten with thankfulness; blankets are spread so that we can lie with our feet to the fire, for we have no tent to cover us to-night; then we join in our evening hymn, which sounds very impressive in this mountain solitude, among the shadows of the everlasting hills, and commending ourselves to the Divine protection, in which petition friends far away are not forgotten, we lie down to rest.

But sleep, at least to some of us, does not come at once. There is too much that is novel and inspiring in our surroundings to admit of that.

"There's a thrill in the air like the tingle of wine,
Or the bugle-blown blast when the scimetars shine ;
And the sky-line is broken by the mountains divine,

Where the planet rises up body-guard before God,
And to cloudland and glory transfigures the sod.
Ah ! to see those grand forms magnificent lift,
' In their sandals of daisies and turbans of drift;
Ah ! to see this dull globe brought sublime to its feet,
Where in mantles of blue the two monarchies meet,
The azure of grace
Bending low in its place.
And this world looking back with a colorless face.
Who marvels Sinai became the State-House of God ?
Who wonders the SERMON down Olivet flowed ?
That the Father and the Son eaeh hallowed a height
Where the lightnings were red and the roses were white ?"

Here the mountains are all about us, their perpendicular cliffs rising to a height of three or four thousand feet, and thought becomes busy with those mighty movements of nature's forces which in ages long distant crumpled up the earth's crust, and heaved these ponderous masses so high in air. And then taking a loftier range meditation becomes sweetly solemn of Him "who by His strength setteth fast the mountains, being girded with power," and who, like "the mountains round about Jerusalem," surrounds His people, a wall of defence forevermore.

We gaze upward through the rift of the cañon and catch a glimpse of the fathomless blue that bends over us, strewn thickly with its golden stars—

"Like some dark beauteous bird, whose plume
Is sparkling with a thousand eyes ;"

and still our thought is of Him "who hath created these things, that bringeth out their host by number ;

He calleth them all by names, by the greatness of His might, for that He is strong in power, not one faileth." And with the heart sweetly resting on the assurance that "the mountains shall depart and the hills be removed, but my kindness shall not depart from thee, neither the covenant of my peace be removed," we—

"Sink in blissful dreams away,
And visions of eternal day."

Next morning finds us somewhat rested from the fatigue of our hard ride, and as we have a short distance farther to go, we are up and away betimes. Half-an-hour's ride brings us in sight of our destination—Long Lake—a beautiful sheet of water some twenty-eight miles long, and of varying width, where we prepare to spend a few short hours. The lake is said to be well supplied with excellent fish, but as we have no boat or raft we are placed at a great disadvantage, and accomplish but little making casts from the shore. However, Chin-a-kee, with a line of deerskin, and a large common hook, manages to secure a good-sized salmon-trout, which agreeably diversifies our dinner bill of fare. Another hour is spent in gazing at the grand, impressive scenery, and then we turn our faces homeward. The ride out is very much like the ride in, only a little more so. To avoid the water, we go through worse thickets than ever. How we got through, retaining a stitch of clothing, will perhaps never be explained. One has to be on the alert every instant. Take care of that hanging branch,

or you may be "single-eyed" for the rest of your life!
Mind that boulder, or your foot may get a twist that
the doctors will not be able to heal in a month! Look
out for that tree, or you may find a case in which the
"bark" is worse than the bite! But where's our
pack-horse? R-r-r-rip! Yes, there he is, just caught
by a snag, and a long rent made through two stout
rubber blankets. Well, we may consider ourselves
fortunate in getting through such a road with no
greater mishap. And here we are at Ghost River
again, sixteen miles from Morley, and a mountain
thunder-storm coming quickly after us. We push on
at greater speed most of the time at a sharp canter,
and after repeated fordings halt at a small clump of
spruce trees just as the first rain drops begin to fall.
Almost before I have time to dismount, McDougall
and the chief have their horses unsaddled; in an
incredibly short space of time the evergreen shelter on
the storm side is thickened by additional boughs, the
waggon-sheet thrown over a pole, a fire kindled, and
by the time the rain is fairly upon us, we are sitting,
figuratively speaking, under our own vine and fig tree,
with supper almost ready. By the time we have refreshed the inner and rested the outer man, the storm
has passed by. Soon, we gladly take our leave of
Ghost River—the most disagreeable ghost I ever met
—and begin to ascend the steep hill, of which mention
has already been made. "Why, McDougall," I said,
"it's impossible for any horse to carry a man up that
hill." "No danger," said he; "you hang on, and he'll

bring you up all right." I "hang on" accordingly; but when half-way up, compassion for my little kayoose prevailed, so I slipped off and led him the rest of the way. That short walk gave me some idea of the method by which house-flies climb up walls and along ceilings.

By 6 p.m, we are on the summit of the hills west of Morley, and turn to take a farewell look at the "mountains divine." We expect to have them in sight for a day or two yet, but shall not again have so near a view as this. Yonder they stand in their rugged grandeur, the storm-cloud wreathed around their shoulders, their summits touched by the rays of the setting sun.

> "The mountain rainbow that gleams before ye,
>   But leaves your solitude doubly bleak ;
> The shadows of sunset falls ghastly o'er ye
>   Cliff frowns upon cliff and peak on peak.
> O Rock of the Desolate, lean and hoary,
>   What lip of man can your grandeur speak ! "

A moment longer let us stand and gaze. Since creation's morning these mountains have towered heavenward like fragments of a petrified eternity, and seem as though they would stand through an eternity to come. Through years that no man can number, yon glorious sun has been dispensing light and heat, but "his eye is not dim, nor his natural force abated;" through periods counted by decades of centuries, this arrowy river beneath our feet has been cleaving its way from its rocky cañon, but its volume is as mighty and its current as swift as when first it began to flow. Yet a time will come when all this will be changed, for " we, according to His promise, look for new heavens and a new earth ;" but "when the mountains have crumbled into ashes, and the judgment flames have licked up the river, and the sun itself is veiled behind the smoke of a burning world," of Him who made them all, it shall be said—"Thy throne, O God, is for ever and ever ;" " from everlasting to everlasting thou art God."

We turn our horses' heads, and in half-an-hour are safe at Morley, very tired (for we have ridden between twenty-five and thirty miles over the worst trail I ever saw), but with pictures hung up in memory's chambers that money could not buy.

## IX.

## AN INDIAN COUNCIL.

N Wednesday forenoon the church bell was rung, and many of the Indians assembled in the school-house for a Council. After some preliminary matters and a few remarks from Bro. McDougall, Mr. Morris, the Government Agent, addressed the Council. He said that, by instructions from the Government, he had been furnishing the Indians with food, but now the supply was very nearly exhausted, and he could not at present obtain any more. He therefore advised them to go to the mountains for the present, and hunt till such time as the produce of their fields would be ready for use. An invitation was then given to the Indians to speak if they desired to do so.

CHIEF JACOB BIG-STONEY said: "I am glad to see one from a far land, especially one who is engaged in a good work. When many of those now present were children, our fathers received the good word. Since then, in poverty and weakness, we have tried to keep it. We entered into it as into a strong place—a place of refuge. Once we trusted in something else, but that something we have put away, and now our trust is in the Great Spirit. When the white men came into our country to treat for our lands, we alone, of all the Indians, were not suspicious; we were ready for the treaty, and we were ready because we had received the good word, and because our Missionary had explained to us what the Government wanted. We believe the white man has great power. We are glad to regard him as our chief; and while we ask his aid for the things of this life, we ask his aid for our spiritual well-being also, because he is wise and strong. We try to do what we are told, and when we say what is good, we think it would be only kindness in the white man to do as we ask. I am glad to see you, and I wish to be remembered to all missionaries and good people in the East."

CHIEF BEAR'S PAW said : " I am glad to see a brother from far, when I know his object in travelling through our country is good. I am *very* glad. In coming to see us they show that they are interested in us, and this encourages me to help myself and my people in what is good. Three years ago, when the treaty was made, I spoke in the same way. I hoped we would have peace, and that whites and Indians would both be benefitted by the treaty. My mind is the same to-day. Sometimes the outlook has been dark. The animals have disappeared ; but I am glad the white man is showing us how to make a living in another way. I hope they will not become weary. I believe it is because of this good religion—because of the interest felt in one another by those who worship alike, that you are with us to-day. We are thankful for that interest, and wish to send through you our thanks to the kind people in your country. We hope they will continue to feel interested in us, and that our homes may still be full of peace. There are two other things I wish to speak about. The first is about the cattle promised by the Government. They were to be delivered two years ago, but we have not seen them yet; and now word comes that our young men must go to Fort McLeod for them. We do not think this is right. We want cattle delivered here on the Reserve, as has been done in the case of other Indians. Besides, if our young men go for the cattle, who will hunt for food while they are gone? I think the advice of the Agent is good : our young men should now go out and hunt. I went out last year, but Mr. McLeod told me to go back to the reserve, as it was near treaty time. Then, when men came this year to survey our reserve, they never asked our wishes in the matter. Why was this? One of our young men has found something in the mountains which he thinks may be gold. Would it be wise for him to take a white man and show him where it is ? "

JAMES DIXON :" I am glad you have come. I am glad our missionary has returned. Our people have tasted enough of the Gospel to know it is the only thing that can save them. We are glad when a mis-

sionary or teacher comes. We see that besides teach-
ing the good word which saves our souls, the white
man wants to save our bodies also. We see this in
what the missionary and the Government have done.
We want to say our thanks, and hope this kindness
will continue. Your kindness has been great and we
are grateful. You see we are poor and weak ; but the
white man is strong. Beside him we feel as little
children. We are glad you are with us, and we are
glad our friends in the East feel an interest in us.
We hope it will continue. When we see a Commis-
sioner or Government Agent, we are glad : when he
gives advice we want to do it. We are thankful to
Mr. Morris [the local agent.] We have no complaint
except about the promised cattle."

CHIEF CHIN-A-KEE : "I agree with all that has been
said by the chiefs. So do our young men. We have
confidence in the Government and in the Great Mother.
It was for our good the treaty was made. We are
thankful, and hope the salvation of our people here and
hereafter will be the result of the white man's interest
in us. But is it our Great Mother's command that
our cattle should be brought to Old Man's river only ?
I cannot believe it. A great thing for us who are
poor would be a small thing for those who are over
their heads in wealth. The Government can do anything. Our strong wish is that the cattle should be
brought here."

GEORGE —— : "I begin where the chief has left off.
I want to be at peace with all the people you may

see in your journey. I hope they will hear what has been said by my brethren to-day. When I first heard about the white man's religion and the Government, and what they would do, I was glad. When the treaty was made, and I knew there would be peace and law in the country, I was *very* glad. When I first listened to the treaty it was very sweet. I have watched closely since then, and some things promised have not come to pass. We were told that so long as we lived and our people lived—so long as the sun shone and the grass grew and the waters ran, this treaty payment would be made. And thus far it has been paid, but the cattle promised us have not come, and the implements have not been such as were promised."

As no others desired to speak, I was asked to say a few words, and spoke in substance as follows : " My friends, I am glad to see you here to-day. We heard in my country that the Stoneys were among the first who listened to the words of the Great Spirit, and because you had received the Gospel you were the friends of the white man and treated him as a brother. We heard that you were loyal to the Great Mother, and were friends of the Government, and the hearts of my people were glad, and they said, The white man and the Stoney will live as brothers, and there will be peace in the land. Then when the treaty was made we were told you were ready, and that your hearts were glad. You were not suspicious, but entered heartily into the matter. And now you are trying to fulfil

your part of the treaty by learning how to cultivate
the soil. I have seen .your fields with growing food,
and have been glad ; for the Stoney cannot live as he
has done in the past. The buffalo are gone, and you
must live more as the white man does. I am sure the
promises made by the Government will be kept ; but
the Government has a great many children, and all
things cannot be done in one day. Sometimes mis-
takes are made, and it takes time to put matters right.
Sometimes the Government may give you food in a
time of distress ; but it is far better you should learn
how to get food for yourselves. When your sons grow
up, you do not always feed them in your lodges ; you
teach them how to hunt and get food for themselves.
If the Government were to feed you it would be only
a little every day ; but if they give you cattle and seed
and implements, you may soon have fruitful fields and
herds of cattle of your own. My people have been
glad to send a missionary and a teacher among you ;
but it will be useless to keep a missionary here unless
you listen to his words, and useless to keep a teacher
unless you send your children to be taught. We hope
to hear from the missionary that all the people listen
to the words of the Great Spirit, and that all your
children go to the school. I have put your words in
my heart, and so has my brother who travels with me.
We both know some of the chiefs of the great Council
at Ottawa, and when we return we will speak your
words in their ears. In days to come, if you wish to
speak to me, tell your words to your missionary, who

will send them to me; and we will know what you think and what you wish."

Bro. McDougall then briefly addressed them in Cree, after which the Council broke up. Another general hand-shaking and "ambu wastage"-ing followed, after which we returned to the mission-house to prepare for our departure on the morrow.

## X.

## MORLEY TO EDMONTON.

UR week of rest and recreation at Morley passed away all to soon; but as only a small part of the journey was yet completed longer delay was out of the question; so on Thursday morning, August 5th, preparations were made for a fresh start. Waggons were loaded, horses brought in and harnessed, and in good season we were ready for the trail. The morning was bright and beautiful, and the weather all that could be desired. With a hearty good-bye to those from whom we were now compelled to separate, and many an "ambu wastage" from the red men who lingered near, we turned our faces eastward, and set out. The hills were clothed in brightest verdure, and the plains adorned with countless flowers of brilliant hues. Brooks of sparkling water, whose source was in the mountains, came leaping down the valleys, hastening to join their tributary streams with the larger current of the Bow whose waters flashed in the sunlight away on our right. Behind us rose the purple mountains, glorious in the cloudless morning light, while before us the foothills sloped onward and downward to the distant plain. It was a lovely sight to which we could not bid farewell without a sigh of regret.

The party now consisted of John and David McDougall, Mr. Nelson and wife, Mr. Warren, and the writer, together with an Indian lad, Myschees by name who attended us as out-rider. Mrs. John McDougall accompanied her husband a few miles on the way. In the course of an hour we reached the banks of our old acquaintance, Ghost River ; but in the bright sunlight of the morning the ghost did not seem nearly so terrible as when we faced it amid the gathering shadows of night. Besides, the water had continued falling during the week, so the crossing was made with comparative ease. In a short time we scaled the steep hill on the eastern side, where pausing a moment we waved a parting adieu to Mrs. McDougall, and then resolutely pushed on. A little after noon we reached our former resting-place on Big Hill Creek, where I proceeded to coax some trout from their shady retreats under the willows. The speckled denizens of the brook were quite willing to bite, but;so were the mosquitoes, who rose in clouds from the long grass beside the stream. However, in spite of the mosquitoes, D. McDougall and the writer secured, in less than half an hour, a string of trout that served the entire party for two meals, with some to spare.

In the course of the afternoon we reached the scene

7

of the runaway accident, and found Bro. McDougall's buck-board just where we left it.   It was speedily taken apart, and packed on one of the waggons to be transported to Edmonton, 200 miles away, the nearest point at which repairs could be effected.   By 7 p.m. we reached our old camping-ground at the Rolling Hills, and pitched our tent for the night.

On resuming our journey, the following morning, we drove to within some two miles of Fort Calgary, then turned to the left, and in a short time struck the main trail leading to Edmonton and the North.   About 11 a.m. we turned off in a westerly direction, and in half an hour reached the bank of a branch of Nose Creek, where we halted for lunch.   After a short rest, D. McDougall and the writer took a buck-board, while J. McDougall and Mr. Warren mounted saddle-horses, and we started on the errand that had brought us out of the way.   After driving a couple of miles we came in sight of a large "hay swamp," lying among the hills. In the rainy season it forms a lake, but now it was dry, and the whole covered with rich grass, about 18 inches high.   The country around is of the kind known as rolling prairie.   It is entirely destitute of trees, not even a bush or shrub being in sight any- where.   Neither of the McDougalls had visited this particular spot before, but they knew the general features of the country, and made their way with a readiness that seemed like instinct.   We first skirted the hay swamp on the north-easterly side, and then round to the south-westerly side.   As we rode along a white object on a gentle slope, some fifty yards from the grassy bed of the lake, met our eye. We rode up and dismounted, and silently, with uncovered heads, stood by a little cairn of stones which alone marks the spot where a half-breed hunter found the lifeless body of the heroic George McDougall. But few words were spoken—only enough to impress the main features of the sad occurrence on the mind—and then with mingled emotions we rode slowly away, pondering on the mysterious Providence that brought our beloved brother to what seemed so untimely an end.

Our visit to the place did not lessen the mystery. Standing on the very spot where the body was found, we had the Rocky Mountains full in view. Now, Bro. McDougall (assuming that the power of vision remained) knew with absolute certainty that these mountains were to the west; facing them, he knew, with equal certainty, that Bow River was on his left, and not very far away; keeping the mountains on the right hand, a straight course would soon bring him to the river, and pursuing a course up the current and towards the mountains for an hour would have brought him opposite Fort Calgary. But it is idle to speculate. We cannot lift the veil of mystery that enshrouds George McDougall's tragic end. We can only rest upon the assurance that what we know not now we shall know hereafter.*

---

* Would it not be a graceful and seemly thing, for those who reverence the work and memory of George McDougall, to unite in providing a plain but enduring monument, to be set up on the spot where his body was found ?—A. S.

THE LATE REV. GEORGE McDOUGALL.

Rejoining the rest of the party we proceeded some distance along the valley of Nose Creek, and ultimately struck the man trail again. During the afternoon we passed over some beautiful fertile plains, and halted for tea at McPherson's Valley, where we found excellent spring water. Barring the lack of timber this is a region well worth the attention of those who may be looking to this part of the North-West as a future home. After tea we drove till well on in the night, and camped amidst clouds of mosquitoes. A vigorous "smudging" afforded relief, however, and we slept in comparative peace.

Our first stage on the following morning took us over the roughest piece of road we had yet travelled. The soil was evidently of first-class quality, but we were beginning to find out that the better the soil the worse the road. The jolting was simply awful, and as my waggon had exceptionally long and good springs, it seemed every few moments as if I would be shot "onward and upward" like a stone from a catapult. That my vertebra was doomed to be shortened by a couple of inches seemed a foregone conclusion ; and matters reached a climax when one of the springs, which had stood the roughest jolting, snapped when we were driving over a comparatively smooth piece of road. Fortunately we were near the halting-place at the "Lone Pine," and after dinner the McDougalls, with a stick of dry poplar and a piece of shaganappi, put all to rights.

We had now passed the treeless region, and henceforth clumps of willow and groves of spruce and poplar were not uncommon. About the middle of the afternoon we rested for a while near a small lake, where we bagged a couple of ducks and half-a-dozen prairie chickens—a welcome addition to the larder. The ducks were shot by Myschees, who borrowed a double-barreled breech-loader from one of the party in order to try his luck. Now, Myschees is not reckoned much of a hunter among his own people; but when bringing in his game he said: "Anybody could be a hunter with a gun like that. You have only to point it toward the ducks, and you are sure to hit some." After tea another stage brought us to the banks of Elk River, where, amid the shadows of evening, we pitched our tents. The country through which we had passed was rich and varied, the growth of pea-vines being unusually abundant.

The Sabbath rest, welcome anywhere, is doubly so on the prairie. When the morning sun lights up the tent, it is so delightful to feel that there is one day on which you can be free from the fatigue and monotony of travel—a day whose hours can be spent in needed rest and profitable meditation ; and when, though hundreds of miles from human habitation, you feel that you can join with "the general assembly and Church of the first-born" in those acts of worship that lifts the soul above the world and time, and bring it near to the gates of Heaven. The very isolation seems to intensify the feeling of devotion, and the sense of utter dependence upon God becomes a felt reality. And in truth God himself seems nearer in these solitudes than " in the city full," for here is nothing to divert the attention or distract the mind, and in the brooding silence the " still small voice " is heard more clearly than amid the din of human activities of the strife of human tongues. Family worship, that beautiful Sabbath morning on the banks or Elk River, both refreshed the spiritual man and revived pleasant home associations, and was a real preparation for the toils of the morrow.

On Monday morning we broke camp in good time, and followed the course of the stream till we reached " McDougall's crossing." At this point the river is about 150 yards wide, but at flood must be at least 200. We could see a boat at the opposite side, tied to a tree; but on trying the ford it was found to be practicable, and we crossed quickly and safely without aid from the boat. On the bank of the river we found a note attached to a stick, which proved to be from Messrs. Glass and Youmans, saying they had crossed safely on the 3rd of August, and had gone forward on the morning of the 4th. Resuming our journey, we drove for some time through groves of poplar and willow for about ten miles, when we forded Blind Man's River, and halted on the bank for dinner. Our second stage took us to Wolf Creek Valley, and our third to Battle River, which we crossed, and three miles farther on camped for the night. The country through which we passed during the day appeared rich and well suited for agriculture, while the water

was good and plentiful, and the timber amply sufficient
for fencing and building purposes.

Our first stage on Tuesday morning took us about
20 miles, and within a short distant of the point where
the trail to Woodville diverges from the one we were
following.    Bro. McDougall and I had arranged to
accompany Mr. Nelson to Woodville, but just at the
point where the trails met we found a tent of Crees,
who told us the Indians had all gone from Woodville
to Edmonton to receive their treaty payments, and
that we would find many of them camped a little
farther on.    Desiring further information, we drove
on, and soon reached a Government Instruction Farm,
in charge of a Mr. Lucas, near which were a number
of Indian tents.    Here the information we had received from the Crees was confirmed, with the additional information that the trail to Woodville was all
but impassable, owing to heavy and long-continued
rains.    We were also told that the Interpreter from
Woodville, D. Whitford, had passed on the way to
Edmonton about two hours before.    As it was useless
to visit the place while the people were all away, it
was decided that Mr. Nelson should camp were he
was, and await the return of Whitford, who would
help him in to Woodville.

We had proceeded but a short distance further, when
I saw a strange looking specimen of humanity coming
to meet us :

" McDougall," I said, " who is that queer looking
mortal ? "

" I declare," he answered. looking up, " that is old Grasshopper ! "

" Well," said I, " if he's a fair sample of the genus, as found in this country, I don't wonder the people dread their appearance. But who is old Grasshopper, anyway ? "

" An old conjuror, of some note among the Crees in his day," was the reply; " and I don't think he is much better yet. But he's coming to see us, and you had better speak to him, or he will feel slighted."

By this time the old man had come up. He gave McDougall a friendly greeting, after which I held out my hand and said :

" How are you, my friend ? I'm glad to see you."

Whereupon a contortion, which doubtless was intended for a smile, passed over the old man's face as he answered :

" Ne duh-duh me non, a-woh-buh-me-don ne no-tā we-tas-ke-mow kah-ke-gow ah-gah-yash-ewh ! "

Of course I didn't. know what he *meant,* but that was what he *said.* However, as he had an ugly-looking scalping knife in his belt, I thought I might as well keep on the safe side, and merely remarked :

" Mr. Grasshopper, those are my sentiments to a hair ! "

When we had driven on a few paces, I said . to McDougall :

" What did the old fellow say, anyway ? "

" Well," said McDougall, laughing, " he said—' I am very glad to see you ; and I want to be friendly with all the Queen's white men."

It was evident that the old man knew there was
" a difference in people."

A few minutes after, we reached a couple of Indian
tents by the wayside.  As we were about passing, two
Indian women came out and walked quickly toward
us.  One of them, with evident emotion, spoke a few
words rapidly in Cree. McDougall replied in the same
tongue, and for a few moments they conversed together.  When we resumed our journey, I turned to
my companion and asked—

" What did that woman say? She seemed to be
deeply moved."

" Yes," he answered, "she *was* moved.  She was a
member of our church at Pigeon Lake, when I was
there; but for some years they have been almost
entirely without a Missionary, and what she said just
now was—' I thank the Great Spirit that I see the
face of a Missionary again.' "

Proceeding on our way, we crossed Big Stone and
Pipe Stone Creeks, and about ten miles farther on
overtook Messrs. Glass and Youmans, camped on
Boggy Plain.  Only those who have experienced the
isolation and loneliness of prairie travel can realize
how glad they were to meet us again.  They received
us with a shout of welcome, and we spent an hour in
talking over our varied experiences since we parted
two weeks before.

On Wednesday morning we drove to White Mud
River, but found the ford too deep for safe crossing,
and turned down the stream for about two miles

the trail leading, for most of the distance, through a
bad swamp. Coming a second time to the river's
bank, we found a bridge composed of poles and brush,
and by careful management got the team safely over,
though *how* the horses managed it without breaking
their legs I shall never be able to explain. The route
for a few miles farther lay through a succession of
swamps, where the travelling was very laborious. We
passed many Indians on their way to Edmonton. A
few had horses, but the greater part were travelling on
foot, while a few had dogs laden with blankets and
camp-kettles, trudging patiently behind their masters.
Farther on we passed several cultivated fields, belonging to Indians, showing that some of them are beginning to settle down as tillers of the soil. Soon our
eyes were gladdened by a sight of the telegraph line
which follows the proposed route of the Canada
Pacific Railway ; and at 4 p.m. we found ourselves on
the bank of the North Saskatchewan, with Fort Edmonton in full view on the opposite side. One of the
Company's inland boats was obtained ; two waggons,
loads and all, were put on board ; and, propelled by
strong arms, the boat was soon at the landing-place.
Our horses had to swim the river, a feat which they
successfully accomplished, although the distance was
considerable and the current pretty strong. Half an
hour later we were kindly received at the hospitable
home of R. Hardisty, Esq., the gentlemanly Chief
Factor of the Hudson Bay Company in the Upper
Saskatchewan District.

## XI.

## EDMONTON TO VICTORIA.

ORT Edmonton occupies a beautiful and commanding site on the north bank of the Saskatchewan River, more than 200 miles below the Rocky Mountains. The most prominent object on the high bank is the Fort of the Hon. Hudson Bay Company,—a large rectangular space, enclosed by a lofty stockade, within which are the stores, shops, offices, &c., of the Company. It is founded as a trading-post more than a hundred years ago, and was for a long time one of the most important in the North-West, being the distributing dèpot for all points north, west, and south. Though not doing the enormous business it once did, it is still a place of considerable importance, and is destined, I think, to be one of the leading centres when the North-West is peopled. The soil of the surrounding country is of excellent quality and exceedingly productive, and the seasons, as a rule, are favorable to the growth of both roots and cereals. There is a settlement extending for several miles along the river, and considerable quantities of wheat and other grains are raised by the settlers. Since my visit there I have learned that a steam thresher has been brought into the neighborhood, and found full employment during the autumn. Two large mills were erected during the summer, one by the H. B. Company, the other (with a saw and shingle mill attached) by a private firm. There are no less than eight stores in the neighborhood, holding in the aggregate, a large amount of goods, and apparently driving a brisk trade. Large seams of coal of fair quality, crop out of the bank not far from the Fort, and can be taken out with great ease. The land in this region is not yet surveyed, and this, of course, retards settlement; but it is said that eighty new settlers went in during the summer of 1880. The course of the Pacific Railway will, doubtless, shape the destiny of many places in the North-West, but should it cross the Saskatchewan at Edmonton, or near there, the latter will yet be a place of great importance.

For many years Edmonton has appeared upon the list of Mission Stations of the Methodist Church; but until within a dozen years it was merely a kind of headquarters to which the missionaries resorted at intervals for supplies, or to obtain occasional tidings from the outside world. It was not till 1871 that buildings were erected, and the place became a mission in fact as well as in name. This work was accomplished through the indefatigable labors of Geo. McDougall, who succeeded in enlisting the co-operation of many residents of the place. In the mission house I saw a book containing a list of subscriptions that would do credit to many a wealthy neighborhood in Ontario. The cost of building at that time was very high, but the only expense to the Missionary Society was a single grant of $400. The premises occupy a beautiful site, half a mile below the Fort, and consist of a church, weather-boarded and painted outside and neatly finished inside ; a comfortable Mission house, a stable, and, surrounding all, a large garden, with a field or two adjoining.

On Sunday, three services were held. I preached, morning and evening, to a congregation numbering over fifty, who listened with attention and with seeming interest. In the afternoon Bro. McDougall preached in Cree to a congregation composed chiefly of Indians and half-breeds, nearly all of whom seemed attentive to the word. One great hindrance to the spread of religion in the North-West is the general disregard of the Sabbath by white men, and this is especially conspicuous in the case of the Mounted Police and Government Agents, who frequently seem to choose Sunday in preference to other days, to set out on journeys ; and this when a start on Monday would answer their purpose equally as well. This has a bad effect on the Indians, and greatly retards efforts for their instruction and enlightenment.

The few days of comparative rest enjoyed at Edmonton were very acceptable ; but a long journey was yet before us, and our stay could not be prolonged.

We found it necessary, however, to make some change in our travelling arrangements. Persons who had just arrived at Edmonton from below, reported the roads in the direction of Victoria as very bad, and the streams to be crossed both high and dangerous ; while our horses which we had driven all the way from Fort Benton, were beginning to show the effects of hard work. But Providence favored us. On the Friday the Company's Steamer *Lily* reached the landing on her upward trip, and it was announced she would leave again the next day. Aftea a brief consultation I sold one of my horses, put the other two with the waggon on board the steamer, and sent them off down the river to Fort Carlton, a distance of over 400 miles by the trail, but following the windings of the river, a distance of over 700. The temptation to accompany them was very great; but several points in the Saskatchewan District had yet to be visited, and I dared not think of home. The Saturday's mail brought me the first letter I had received since leaving Toronto eight weeks before ; and though it was written only three days after my departure, it brought up home associations so vividly that it required no small amount of resolution to let the steamer depart without me. But at length she steamed away, and I turned to my work.

Our horses being gone, some other mode of travel had to be devised. Of course, we had foreseen this, and made our arrangements accordingly. From Mr. Hardisty we obtained a large flat-bottomed boat, into which we put harness, camping utensils, tent, provisions, &c., and prepared to boat down the river, a distance of some 700 miles. Bro. J. McDougall, Mr. Warren, the Indian lad Myschees, and myself, constituted the crew. Shortly after noon on Monday we were ready. Some of our kind friends accompanied us to the landing, and with a cordial good-bye we pushed off, and went floating down the stream. Soon the last tokens of settlement or civilization disappeared from view, and the lonely part of this strange journey was fairly begun. To float with the current, with a bright sky overhead, was pleasant enough ; but that rate of speed would not answer, so there was nothing for it but to take to the oars. The boat was heavy and the oars were long, and rowing even with the current in our favor was no joke ; while rowing against a strong head-wind, which was a common occurrence, was so much like a day's work with a buck-saw that no one but an expert could have told the difference, and I imagine *he* would have considered the difference to be in favor of the buck-saw. Regarded as a mere amusement this sort of travelling is not a success,—it is difficult to see just where the laugh comes in ; but as a cure for dyspepsia and loss of appetite, it may be relied upon with tolerable certainty.

About twenty miles below Edmonton is Fort Saskatchewan, a post of the Mounted Police. We purposed making a short stay at this point as we heard that a Methodist family from Ontario had settled in the neighborhood; but our progress was delayed 'by a heavy thunderstorm that came up during the latter part of the afternoon. A strong wind blew up the river, and the rain descended in torrents for nearly an hour. We tried to provide a little shelter by throwing the waggon-sheet over a horizontal pole, but the rain was so copious that it seemed to go through everything, and drenched the crew pretty thoroughly. The storm delayed us over an hour, so that it was after dark when we reached Fort Saskatchewan, and as we had no way-marks to guide us to the house we wanted to find, we did not attempt to land, but continued our course down the stream.

As we could not spare time to camp on shore arrangements had been made to sleep on board. Some rugs, &c., were spread on the bottom of the boat, on which we curled ourselves up—there was hardly room to stretch—and letting the boat drift with the current, went to sleep. In this part of the Saskatchewan boulders are pretty numerous, and it was arranged that Myschees should keep watch during the middle of the night, lest we should run on a rock. About midnight I awoke, and heard the roar of water dashing over boulders some distance below. I looked round for Myschees, and there he was propped against a roll of bedding sleeping most serenely. I spoke in an undertone to McDougall, who woke on the instant and seizing one of the long oars managed with a few strokes to turn us out of the course of a large boulder, that came to the surface right in the middle of the

8

stream. This danger past, we lay down again, and nothing more occurred during the night to disturb our slumbers.

Next day the weather was pleasant, and as a fair wind was blowing down the river, the waggon-sheet was transformed into a sail, which greatly aided our progress, and relieved us from the fatigue of rowing. During the day a small flock of wild geese were seen in the bend of the river, and after several unsuccessful attempts I managed to bag one. About 3 p.m. we reached Victoria, and were kindly received by the Rev. J. A. McLachlen and his estimable wife. The garden attached to the Mission house showed something of the capabilities of the soil. Potatoes, peas, beans, carrots, cabbages, tomatoes, &c., were thriving apace, while beds of pansies, and other favorites, showed Mrs. McLachlen's care, and gave a delightful home-look to the surroundings.

This Mission, too, is a creation of the McDougalls. When George McDougall first visited the country in 1862, he found Mr. Woolsey at Smoking Lake, some 30 miles north from the river, where he had just erected a little cabin, and proposed to locate a Mission. Bro. McDougall was convinced that a spot on the bank of the river was a much better location, and resolved to begin a mission there, though strongly dissuaded by others on the ground that the place selected was right in the war-path of the Blackfeet. In the meantime John McDougall had gone to visit some other points, and on his return, father and son were to consult about the work to be done; but the H. B. boats coming down the river, the father had to leave, and when John reached the spot he found merely a stick with a piece of paper attached containing the brief and Spartan-like message—"Good-bye, my son ; do your duty, and God will bless you." It was a trying situation for a young man not yet out of his teens, to be thrown on his own resources, more than a thousand miles from friends and home, alone in a vast wilderness, and surrounded on all sides by savage Indians ; but after the first burst of uncontrollable emotion, he went bravely to work to assist Mr. Woolsey, while Mr. Steinhauer came from Whitefish Lake, sixty miles away, to render further aid; and when George McDougall returned from Norway House with his family the following summer, he found a Mission house well on toward completion, and a good deal of material ready for a church. As in other cases the lumber had all to be cut by hand. But here a heavy loss befell the party. Part of the logs and timber had been prepared about six miles up the river, and were all ready for rafting, when a prairie fire seized upon and consumed the whole, and the work had to be done over again.

From 1863, Victoria has continued on the list of Methodist missions, and for several years flourished greatly. At one time there were no less than six classes, two composed of Indians, the others of whites and half-breeds. Since then, however, owing to frequent changes, vacancies and unsuitable appointments, the cause languished; but is now reviving. Bro. McLachlen and his wife are doing well, and getting a firm hold upon the people, who were much alarmed when a rumor got abroad among them that their Missionary was likely to be removed.

The establishment of a Mission at Victoria was the signal for others to come on the ground. The H. B. Company built a trading-post of considerable extent, and a number of half-breed families from Red River came up and made their homes in the immediate neighborhood. The site is a good one, and Victoria may be a place of importance in the future. The Mission premises consist of a house and barn, and a small church, which in the past was also used as a school-house. In addition to the garden there used to be a large field or two enclosed and cultivated; but the fences have fallen down or been carried away, and now there is but an open common. It is painful to witness these signs of neglect in connection with a Mission upon which so much has been expended; but I have good hopes that in this respect also there will now be a change for the better. We were sadly reminded of the trials of former missionaries at this place by seeing in the Mission-house garden the graves of the wife and two sisters of John McDougall, who fell victims to the terrible scourge of small-pox when last it swept through that country. What added to the painfulness of the bereavement was the fact that Bro. McDougall was absent from home when his wife died. He had been away on a Missionary tour as far as Pigeon Lake, and had reached Edmonton on his return; but just as he entered the Fort by one gateway, a messenger entered by the other, bringing the sad tidings that his wife had passed away.

## XII.

## VICTORIA TO WHITEFISH LAKE AND BACK.

N Wednesday, August 18th, I set out, in company with Bros. McDougall and Mc-Lachlen, to visit Whitefish Lake, a Mission station sixty miles north-east from Victoria. On this route we noticed a considerable change in both timber and soil. Poplar bluffs, growing on rich black soil, were still the main feature, but in some places we passed through extensive groves of cypress pine, where the soil was a light sand, unfit for general cultivation, but producing vast quantities of cranberries, the bright scarlet fruit and glossy leaves covering the ground in many places like a variegated carpet. Rolling hills alternated with level stretches of low ground, covered with willow, while in other places the trail crossed extensive hay-swamps, where the water for a long distance together came up to the bellies of the horses. The country is well watered with running streams, and if it will only admit of drainage in the lower portions, may yet possess considerable value.

For weeks past heavy showers had been frequent, a very unusual circumstance at this season of the year. As a consequence we found the trail bad in places, and some of the streams difficult to cross; but by dint of perseverence we made fair progress, and camped at night on a grassy knoll, near a running stream. The sky was covered with heavy clouds and the rain came down at intervals, giving the surroundings a sombre appearance. To go off through the long wet grass to the nearest willow copse in search of dead wood for our fire, was not a very agreeable task; but when the fire got headway, and we sat in its glow, beneath our tent, discussing a liberal supply of bacon and potatoes, washed down with a cup of steaming tea, things began to look brighter, and we concluded there might be worse circumstances in life than camping on the prairie, although in the midst of a pouring rain.

Next day the weather was better, but the roads were none of the best. Just before halting for dinner we passed through an extensive hay-swamp. The grass was very tall and rank, and the water in some places came above the bottom of our buckboard. It was evident the rains had been excessive, for in many places where stacks of hay had stood on dry ground last summer, there was now from one to two feet of water. In fact the Indians and others have been obliged this season to get their supply of hay from the hillsides and higher levels, the amount of water in the swamps rendering work there impossible. In these hay-swamps wild ducks are very abundant. To shoot them is easy, but to get them out afterwards is another thing.

Early in the afternoon we came in sight of Goodfish Lake, and soon after reached the outskirts of the settlement to which we were going. Indian houses and fields could be seen in various directions, indicating a good degree of civilization, and showing what can be accomplished by faithful missionary effort even in a few years. When near the Mission we passed by as fine a herd of cattle, belonging to the Indians, as one need wish to see. About four p.m. we reached the Mission house, and were welcomed by Bro. Steinhauer, the Missionary in charge. As the Mission and settlement have grown up entirely under his labors, some account of the man will not be out of place.

The REV. H. B. STEINHAUER is an Ojebway Indian, having been born near Rama about 1820. About this time Elder Case began his apostolic work among the native tribes. In pursuit of his benevolent design he visited many places in the United States, Philadelphia among the rest, where a family named Steinhauer resided. They became deeply interested in Case's work among the Indians in Canada, and having lost by death a little boy of their own, to whom they were much attached, they authorized Mr. Case to pick out a promising Indian youth, and have him educated at their expense. In 1828 a great awakening took place among the Indians, and the

REV. H. B. STEINHAUER.
(*Indian Missionary at Whitefish Lake.*)

same year 133 were baptized at Holland Landing, among whom was the subject of this sketch, who received the name of Henry Steinhauer, after the gentleman already referred to. The following year Mr. Case took young Henry to the school he had established at Grape Island; he also took him, in company with young Allan Salt, and several other Indian youths, on a tour through parts of the United States, where, by singing at Missionary Meetings, they excited a great deal of interest.

After remaining a year or two at Grape Island, young Steinhauer was sent to Cazenovia Seminary, where he remained three years, making commendable progress in his studies. He then returned to Canada and taught school for two years at the Credit Mission. Subsequently, he spent some time with his mother at Lake Simcoe, and in 1835 went to Upper Canada Academy, which he left the following year to teach school at the Alderville Mission. In the spring of 1840 he left Alderville to accompany the Rev. James Evans to the North-West, but was left by that devoted Missionary at Lac la Pluie, as Interpreter to the Rev. W. Mason, who had been sent to that point by the English Society. Bro. Steinhauer continued in this capacity for several years and then, by Mr. Evans' instructions, he went on to Norway House, where he served as Teacher and Interpreter till the year 1850. He was next sent to Oxford House to begin a Mission, where he spent four years, and then came back to Norway House to take temporary charge of the

Mission, where he spent four years, the Rev. Mr. Mason
having gone over to the Church of England.   He
remained at his post till the arrival of the Rev. Thos.
Hurlburt in the autumn of the same year, the Rev.
Mr. Brooking being appointed at the same time to
Oxford House.

During the summer of 1854 the Rev. John Ryerson
visited the Missions in the Hudson Bay Territory.
He took Bro. Steinhauer with him to York Factory,
from which point they sailed in a Company's ship to
England, reaching that country in October.   Leaving
again in December, they reached Canada before
Christmas.

At the London Conference of 1855 Bro. Steinhauer
was ordained, and sent, with the Rev. Thomas Woolsey,
to the far North-West, to carry on the work that
Rundle had begun.   Woolsey made Edmonton his
head-quarters, while Steinhauer went to Lac la Biche.
He remained there till June, 1857, when he went to
Whitefish Lake, and pitched his tent where the
school-house of the Mission now stands.   Here he has
since remained, working with a cheering measure of
success.   He has gathered around him a community of
Christian Indians, of the Cree nation, whose conversion
and subsequent lives have been a signal proof of the
power of the Gospel.   During the twenty-three years
that have elapsed since the founding of the Mission,
many have died in the faith of Christ, and many now
living are witnesses of his saving power.   Bro. Steinhauer also led the way in civilization, showing the

First Religious Service at Whitfish Lake.

Indians how to build houses, and enclose and cultivate fields.

In another matter Bro. Steinhauer has rendered signal service to the cause of God among the Crees. When the Rev. James Evans went to the North-West, in 1840, he was already meditating the possibility of reducing the Cree tongue to writing. In this he succeeded, by inventing what is known as the Syllabic Characters: a system so wonderfully simple and adapted to the tongue, that an Indian of fair intelligence can, by two or three days' application, read in his own tongue the Word of God. Mr. Evans not only invented the characters but cut the first type in which an attempt was made to print them. Soon after, the work of translating the Scriptures began, and it was in this work that Bro. Steinhauer rendered efficient service in conjunction with John Sinclair, a half-breed, afterwards employed as a Native Assistant at Oxford House. Mr. Sinclair translated the Old Testament as far as the end of Job, also the Gospels and Acts; while Mr. Steinhauer translated from the beginning of the Psalms to the end of the Old Testament, and from the beginning of Romans to the end of the New.

The MS. of these translations was entrusted to the Rev. Mr. Mason, who was now a Missionary of the Church of England at York Factory. He took it to England, where the work of printing was undertaken by the British and Foreign Bible Society. When the work was passing through the press, Mr. Mason, with characteristic modesty but very questionable morality, had his own name printed on the title-page as the translator of the work. Subsequently, after the death of James Evans, Mason claimed to be the inventor of the Syllabic Characters, and within a couple of years the writer has seen the claim asserted in his behalf in an English paper.

The Mission premises at Whitefish Lake consist of the house in which the Missionary resides, and a building used for a school-house and church: The latter building had become rather dilapidated, and two or three years ago the Indians made preparations to build a new church. The walls of the building were erected, but they have been unable to finish it, and help from some quarter will be indispensable. The buildings occupy a site on a rise of ground near the south end of the lake, some three or four hundred yards from the shore. The lake itself is about twelve miles long by four miles wide, and contains an abundant supply of whitefish of superior quality. Several small fields adjoining the Mission are well cultivated, and the garden gave very satisfactory evidence of the fertility of the soil. About half of the latter enclosure was sown with grain, which at the time of my visit was heading out. The Missionary asked me if I knew what it was. "Well," I said, "it is either wheat, or oats, or barley ; I can't tell which, as there seems to be about an equal quantity of each, not counting the weeds, which are very abundant." "Just so," said he ; "and yet that field was sown with some of the Government seed that was supplied to the Indians last year."

Who wouldn't be a contractor for Indian supplies ?

On Friday morning we held a meeting in the little Mission Church, which was well filled, although the day was wet. Bro. McDougall opened the service, and afterwards I gave an address, McD. interpreting. As this was the only opportunity I was likely to have, I gave a general address, mingling counsel and exhortation. The meeting was then thrown open, and an opportunity given to those present to say what they wished. After a brief pause,

O-MUSH-KA-GO (B. Sinclair) said: "Sometimes I forget what I want to say; but one thing I can't forget— what the Gospel has done for me. And since I received it I have been willing to help in any way, even sweeping the house of the Lord. Missionaries sent me into this country, and I helped them as I could ; and when this Mission was established I resolved to settle here. I was very glad when Bro. Steinhauer came, and I have remained here ever since. In the absence of the Missionary, I have tried to tell the people what I know of the Gospel. Many of the fathers heard the Word, and some did not; but many of those who heard have since died happy in the Lord. Now that our Missionary is going away for a time, I will gladly do what I can. I am thankful for the interest which the people in Canada feel in us."

MOI-GAH-DISH (Nathaniel Leg): "I am thankful to-day for what you have told us about the feelings of the friends in the East. I know the Lord listens to prayer; He has heard prayer for me. We were many brothers—now all are dead but two; but the Lord heard prayer and comforted us in sorrow. I am glad to hear that friends pray for us, and I send greetings to them, although I may never see them. Tell Bro. Campbell that I remember him, and that I received good from his Ministry. Another thing: these houses [Mission house and church] were built by Mr. Steinhauer; but he is getting old. We see the need of a new church. We have the walls of one up. Where do we look for help to finish it? To our friends in the East."

KO-PWE-WE-YAT (Samuel Jackson): "I am very thankful for the religion of Jesus Christ. I was as those you told us about—had no knowledge of God. But when the Missionaries came I heard the Word, and got more and more light; and now I am trying to do what you told us—hold fast to Jesus Christ. I am glad the Gospel came to us and told us it was not the will of God that any should perish. I am trying to live for this, that I may serve God here and go to Him when I die. I am very glad to hear of so many kind friends in the East who are trying to serve God; and I feel that they are my friends. I hope to meet you at last in the Great Kingdom."

PETER APON : " If we were met to talk about anything else, I would say nothing; but when it is about what the Gospel has done, I can speak out about what Jesus has done for me. As you told us, I want to hold

fast.   One reason I know how good religion is, I
have had much trouble, and it has comforted and sus-
tained me.   When I meet a Missionary, I feel at once
—here is my friend.   It is my strong desire to follow
the teachings of Jesus Christ."

CHIEF BUH-CANN: "Others have been talking about
religion; here am I also.   Why should I sit still?   It
is the Lord's doing.   Ever since I can remember I
have been the friend of the white man; and those many
friends in your country—I shake hands with them
from my heart.   One thing I would like: in case of
Mr. Steinhauer or any other Missionary returning, I
would like he could have a supply of medicines to use
among the people."

GEORGE: "I want to ask questions.   We are scattered
along Whitefish and Goodfish Lakes.   I do not com-
plain of any one; but I ask for information.   It is a long
way from this Mission, and we cannot all come here to
service, nor our children to school.   I thought this
the time to speak about it.   Is it our duty to come all
that way to service?   Mr. Steinhauer is now getting
old, and it is hard for him to go to Goodfish Lake to
give us service."

Further devotional services now followed, and the
meeting was brought to a close.   After the meeting,
an incident was related to me, which may be worth
recording:   In the settlement there is a young Indian
named Adam, a member of a once numerous family.
He is perhaps 19 years of age, but is too feeble and
sickly to do anything for his own support.   At inter-

vals during the last ten years or so, his mother, brothers, and sisters have been successively removed by death; and a few weeks before I visited the place, his father also passed away. Speaking of his lonely condition after his father's death, he said: "I was sitting alone one day, thinking of all the trouble I had passed through, and how very sad it was to be left all alone, sick and poor. But as I was thinking, it seemed to me the door opened. I looked up, and there stood the most beautiful person I had ever seen. He stood a little while looking at me with great pity and tenderness, and then said: 'My child don't be so sad, because your friends are gone. Years ago I came and took your mother; then after that I took your brothers and sisters, one by one; last of all I took your father; and if you are faithful to me a little longer I will come for you also, and take you to my beautiful home, where your father and mother and brothers and sisters are all gathered, and there will be no more hunger or sorrow or sickness or loneliness, forever.' When I looked again," said Adam, "the stranger was gone; but my sorrow was gone also, and now I don't feel sad or lonely any more." "But," says some incredulous reader, "the poor lad was only dreaming." Perhaps so; but, hearing his story, I could not but repeat softly the Master's words: "Thou hast hid these things from the wise and prudent, and hast revealed them unto babes."

Shortly after noon on Friday, we left Whitefish Lake, accompanied by Bro. Steinhauer, who is going

9

to Ontario for a season. The weather was rather
better than on the outward trip, but there was the
same amount of mud and water to go through. As we
were crossing one of the hay swamps already mentioned, we passed through what had been the enclosure
of a hay stack; but the water now covered the spot to
a depth of some two-and-a-half feet. Just at the
deepest place, a projecting rail caught in the spokes of
our buckboard, and brought us to a dead halt. Now,
when a horse is stopped in deep mud or water, he generally manifests a perverse disposition to lie down;
and our horses, or one of them, were no exception to
the rule. But a lie down at that point would probably have involved a break of some kind, and the
necessity of jumping, waist deep, into a pond of vil-
lainous-smelling slush, at a distance of several hundred
yards from the nearest firm ground, and to this we
were not disposed to submit without a struggle. I
accordingly devoted my attention to the horse, and
managed, by a vigorous use of reins and whip, to keep
him on his feet, while McDougall seized a hatchet, and
by a few well-directed blows cut the rail in two and
set us free. A drive of some twenty-five miles used
up the available daylight, and we camped for the
night. The next day, about 4 p.m., we reached Victoria, and again took up our quarters at the mission
house.

On Sunday we held two services. I preached in
the morning to an attentive congregation, and in the
afternoon McDougall preached in Cree to a well-filled

house. During our stay the accounts we had heard at Edmonton about the state of the roads between that point and Victoria were confirmed. The Rev. Dr. Newton, Episcopalian minister, arrived on Friday, and reported that in crossing Sucker Creek he and his horse barely escaped with their lives. And this is the kind of travelling that missionaries and others in the North-West experience almost continually.

## XIII.

## BOATING DOWN THE SASKATCH-
## EWAN.

N Monday, August 23rd, we prepared to bid
farewell to our friends at Victoria. It took
some time to get our effects carried down
the bank to the river, and stowed away in
the boat. As McDougall must now leave us
to return to his work at Morley, and the rest
of us knew nothing of the route toward Winnipeg, a
guide became indispensable. After some enquiry I
engaged an old H. B. freighter and steersman—Sam
Favel, to wit—who proved a valuable help on the
journey. Having several children at Red River, he
was the more willing to go, and for his board and a
moderate compensation, agreed to make the through
trip. At a quarter-past two everything was in readiness, and our friends came down to the bank to see us
off. Our party had been steadily thinning out at
various points, and now we were to part from Bro. Mc-
Dougall, upon whom we had relied in every emergency

during the journey. Before us lay a distance of some 600 miles down what was to us an unknown river, and after that, 600 miles more before we would reach railway communication, or hear from those we had left at home. From this point it devolved upon me to command the little expedition; and there is all the difference imaginable between following the lead of some one familiar with the country and the modes of travel, and having to shoulder the responsibility and decide every point yourself. Once more the thought of the isolation to which many of our mission families are subjected came forcibly to my mind, and I could better appreciate the strength of purpose which holds them faithful to their work. A little over a year ago, Mrs. McLachlen had gone out to Victoria a bride, with no white woman within eighty miles of the station. As she stood on the river bank watching our preparations for departure, she knew we were going almost to the very home of her childhood, and I doubt not the yearning must have been strong in her heart for an opportunity to see her friends again ; but no word betrayed the desire, and only a tear-dimmed eye told that the feeling was there.

At last all things were ready. Warren, Steinhauer, and the guide were in the boat. I stood a moment longer on the shore, while in few but earnest words we commended each other " to God and to the word of His grace." Then with a cordial grasp of the hand, and a mutual " God bless you! " we pushed out into the stream. For a while we let the boat drift with the current, and sat looking back at our friends on the shore; but in a little while a bend of the river hid them from our view, and we felt we were fairly on the way. There was no longer sight or sound of human habitation. The great Saskatchewan was beneath us, its wooded banks on either hand, a strip of blue sky overhead, and that was all.

Before leaving Victoria we made enquiry about the river and were informed that, with the exception of " Crooked Rapid," about forty miles farther down, and numerous sand-bars at intervals, we were not likely to meet any serious difficulties in navigating the stream. Being anxious to pass the rapid by daylight we bent to the oars, and pulled pretty steadily during the rest of the afternoon; but darkness came down and the rapid was not yet reached. A faint breeze was blowing up the river, and as the darkness deepened, the hoarse roar of the rapid came distinctly to our ears. The wooded banks of the river both conveyed and intensified the sound, and made the rapid seem stronger than it really was. A good deal, too, depends upon the state of the water in the river, the current of the rapid being much more broken at some seasons than at others. We now consulted as to what had better be done. Prudence—or some other feeling —said it would be safer to pull ashore and tie up till morning; but in that case some eight hours time would be lost, which was a serious consideration.

"Sam," I said, addressing the guide, "what do you think of it?"

"I think we can manage it, sir," he answered. "If
we can only keep clear of a stray boulder or the like,
there will not be much danger."

We could tell, by the quickening of the current, and
the increasing sound, that we must be near the spot.
In a short time we reached the bend of the river that
gives name to the rapid. It was now too late to think
of landing, and down we must go. An anxious gaze
was bent down the stream, where, between the darkly
wooded banks,

> " The white-caps dancing through the night,
> Gave to tho strained and eager eye
> A wild and shifting light."

In the faint starlight it was impossible to tell what
boulders or other dangers might be in the way. But
there was little time for thought. In a few moments
we were in the midst of the rapid, where our heavy
boat danced about like a canoe; but Sam had the
steering oar, and kept her bow down, and in a very
short time, though it seemed long to us, we were past
the rapid, and floating in a quiet current. As we had
no reason to expect any similar experience again during the night, we prepared to rest, and let the boat
drift as she would.

There is a weird solemnity in the surroundings.
Moonlight there is none, and the stars cast only a faint
uncertain shimmer on the gliding water. The poplar
groves come down to the waters' edge, and hem us in
between walls of impenetrable gloom,

> "While, with a sorrowful deep sound,
> The river flows between."

Other sound there is none, save when at intervals, with startling suddenness, the sepulchral note of a night-owl calling to his fellow, or the human-like moan of a beaver, echoes across the stream. We are far from human habitation; and unless some wandering Indian has pitched his tent among the poplars, and, for aught we know, may be peering out of his leafy ambush as we go floating by, we are as completely isolated as if we were out in the middle of the sea. And yet there is something in the very stillness, and in the quiet murmur of the waters that soothes like the touch of a cool, soft hand upon a fevered brow. We are "near to Nature's heart," and the encompassing darkness is like the shadow of a brooding wing, beneath which we sink peacefully to rest. At daylight next morning we were still drifting, and we estimated that since we rested from the oars, after running Crooked Rapid, we had drifted with the current some five-and-twenty miles.

Shaking ourselves from slumber we took again to the oars. On reaching a suitable place, where we saw some dead timber on the bank, we landed, kindled a fire, and put on the kettle. A few minutes sufficed to cook some bacon and prepare a kettle of tea, and then jumping into the boat we pushed off, and ate our morning meal while floating down the stream. It is only by "redeeming the time" in this way that satisfactory progress can be made on such a journey. The rule is not to travel fast, but to keep at it. Soon after breakfast a strong wind began to blow up the river, and in a short time rain began to fall. We soon found that very little head-way could be made, and that our best plan would be to camp till the weather cleared. Accordingly we pulled ashore, tied up the boat, carried tent and other necessaries up a steep bank, and formed a camp under the lee of a clump of willows. The wind continued with unabated force, and the rain fell without intermission throughout the day and the following night. During the afternoon the temperature lowered, and snow mingled with the rain.

On Wednesday morning, the 25th, it was still raining, but towards noon the weather cleared somewhat, and after dinner we resumed our voyage, having been detained in camp about thirty hours. Showers fell at intervals through the afternoon, but the wind abated, and we made fair progress. When darkness fell we prepared to rest, and allowed the boat to drift as usual About the middle of the night I awoke, and lifting my head took a survey of the situation. The sky had cleared and the stars were shining. I found we had entered a current more swift than usual, and I could hear a sound ahead that I knew was caused either by a pretty strong rapid, or else by the dash of water over boulders in the channel. Springing up I seized an oar, thinking it safest to keep the boat with her bow down stream. Peering through the darkness I could faintly discern some object ahead, but whether an island or a sudden bend in the river, I could not tell. The mystery was soon solved. The object was an island in the middle of the stream, and before I had time to change my course, the boat struck on the gravelly beach with a force that nearly took me off my feet, and woke up the rest of the crew in a hurry. But no damage had been done; the boat swung round into the channel, and we floated on as before.

Thursday morning found us still floating down the river. The weather continued much the same as the previous day,—flying showers at intervals, but the breeze still up the stream, which prevented the use of a sail. About 11 a.m. we met the steamer *Lily* on her upward trip. The captain courteously stopped, and took on board a parcel and several letters for Victoria. The scenery on this part of the Saskatchewan is beautifully park-like,—bluffs of timber, interspersed with stretches of open prairie, sloping up from the river, and often resembling cultivated fields, with hedge-rows and small clumps of ornamental shrubbery. About 4 p.m. we reached Fort Pitt, having been about 44 hours on the way from Victoria, exclusive of the 30 hours spent in camp. Fort Pitt is in charge of William McKay, Esq., a thorough citizen of the country, having been born at Fort Ellice over half a century ago, and never out of the country to this day. He received us with much kindness, and invited us to stay for tea, an invitation which we gladly accepted. Mrs McKay has a garden, which illustrates the productive powers of the soil of this part of the North-West. Cabbages, celery, radishes, tomatoes, squash, cucumbers, onions, kale, red pepper, corn, etc., etc., showed a luxuriant growth; while beds of petunias and portulacca bloomed in masses, with great richness of coloring.

Soon after 6 p.m. we were again at our oars, and in two minutes ran on a sand-bar. A little pushing, and and a good deal of puffing, got us off, and we avoided any more mishaps of the kind. As the night was cloudy, we lay down soon after 8 p.m., and went to sleep, letting the current take us whither it would. Fortunately the water was high—an unusual thing at this season of the year,—and we drifted all night without touching a sand-bar or other obstruction. When morning broke we were still making progress at about four miles an hour; but we had now become so accustomed to this kind of locomotion that we no longer considered it necessary to ask, in the language of the average political newspaper—"Whither are we drifting?"

*August* 27.—Pulled ashore early and boiled the kettle, and at 7 a.m. resumed the oars. The sky is still somewhat cloudy, but there are patches of blue, and cheerful glimpses of sunshine,—a pleasing change after so many days of rain. During the day we passed a number of beautiful islands, most of them wooded with poplar or green with willow to the water's edge, while occasional clumps of spruce gave a pleasing variety to the scene.

At a point where the river was at least three quarters of a mile wide, we were pulling down midstream, when we noticed a tiny dark object on the surface of the water. As we got nearer we saw it was alive, and when within a boat's length were astonished to see a little mouse, his tail curved in the air, actually *swimming in the river!* Reaching out a narrow piece of board, I lifted him gently and quickly from the water and held him aloft. He looked rather astonished at first, but quickly adapted himself to circumstances, and proceeded to brush his fur and dry himself in the sunshine with evident satisfaction. As we neared the next point we pulled in shore, and as I reached over with the board our little mariner sprang to the bank, and scampered away into the grass.

In this part of the river sand-bars are numerous. As we were passing one of these we saw some animal moving about in the shoal water, and a nearer view showed it to be a badger, resting a little midway of the river. Sam having expressed a wish for some badger grease for culinary purposes, I took a long shot with my Winchester rifle. The bullet struck the water just behind the badger, and thinking something was after him he plunged into deeper water and began swimming toward the boat. A better aim at shorter range was more successful, and giving a single plunge he went to the bottom like a stone. The water was not very deep, but was too muddy for anything to be seen at the bottom, so we had to pull on again empty handed.

Passing among some of the islands, signs of beaver became numerous. We saw where trees and branches had been gnawed off, and well beaten paths led down the banks. Just as it was getting dusk I saw a beaver's lodge some distance ahead, and a beaver moving in the water close by. We let the boat drift, and

I was just raising the rifle to my shoulder when two big fellows, who had been sitting on the lodge among the shadows, plunged suddenly into the water. While we were watching to see if they would re-appear, I glanced down stream, and saw a noble fellow swimming across, about twenty yards away. I took a quick shot, but aimed too well, for the bullet struck him in the head and he sank like a stone. We were much disappointed at not securing the prize, as our stock of meat was getting low

Drifting at night was now becoming risky, on account of the numerous sand-bars. Besides, we did not know how near we might be to Battleford, and we did not want to pass it unawares in the night; so about 8 p.m. we tied up to a clump of willows and went to sleep. During the night a beaver swam near the boat with his peculiar moaning call, but before I could lift my rifle he plunged under the water.

On Saturday, the 28th, we got off at daybreak, and pulled against a head-wind, which gradually increased till it was almost a gale. This made rowing very laborious work; but about 1 p.m. we reached the mouth of Battle River, and a pull of two miles against the stream, brought us to Battleford, the capital of the North-West Territory. As it was our invariable custom to rest on the Sabbath, we prepared to camp. A clear spot was found on the vacant lot of the H. B. Co., where we pitched our tent; our movables were soon brought up from the boat, and we got matters into shape for the day of rest. During the night rain came on again, and continued for most of the next day.

## XIV.

### BATTLEFORD TO PRINCE ALBERT.

**B**ATTLEFORD is not the handsomest place in the world. The natural features of the country are good, and the view from the hill near the Governor's residence is commanding, but the little town itself is homely enough. The buildings—about 15 or 20 in number—are log structures, most of them mere shanties, some with thatch and some with mud roofs, only one being shingled, This part of the town is situate on a level bottom, on the south side of Battle River, and is the centre of a considerable trade. Across the stream is the point between the Battle and the Saskatchewan Rivers, a beautiful prairie plateau, lofty and dry, upon which is located the police barracks. Why this plateau was not selected as the site of the town I cannot imagine. It strikes a stranger as immeasurably superior to the one chosen. On a hill south of the business part of the town are the residences of the Governor, the Stipendiary Magistrate, the

Registrar and other public functionaries. These structures appear to be well built, and resemble the average class of residences in Ontario towns.

The population of Battleford is about 300. One-half are claimed by the Catholic Church, the rest are nominally Protestants; but at the time of my visit there was no regular Protestant service in the place. A school-house built on the "union" principle, is available for religious services, and both Anglicans and Presbyterians have occupied it at intervals; but there is no church in the place, if we except a log shanty used as a chapel by the Roman Catholics. This latter body is making tremendous efforts for supremacy, and is working, as it always does, for the future. I may remark here that although Battleford has been the capital of the North-West Territories for a number of years past, the town-plot has not yet been surveyed, hence a squatter's claim is the only title by which property can at present be held. The Church of Rome, taking advantage of this, has built its little log chapel, and on the ground of occupancy is claiming I am told, thirty acres in what will be the town-plot. If they claim it they will assuredly get it; for under our wretched system of party government, the Church of Rome holds the balance of power; neither party can retain a working majority in the Dominion Parliament without Catholic votes, and these will always be given to the party who yields most readily to the demands of the Church. The determination of Rome to gain the ascendancy if possible in the North-West is manifest in the efforts she is making to control the public offices. It is true the present Governor is a Protestant, but his private Secretary is a Catholic; the Registrar is a Catholic; the Sheriff (I am not sure if this is the correct official designation) is a Catholic; and I was informed that just before I visited Battleford, two Protestant Farm Instructors in the vicinity had been dismissed, and two Catholic French Canadians put in their places,

The soil in the vicinity of Battleford is not equal to that lying either to the east or the west. To the south-ward I am told there are tracts of sandhills that are not likely to be of permament value, and will never be suitable for cultivation ; but these tracts are not very extensive, and as to the rest, the land may be said to be of very fair quality. It is only in comparison with the rich black soil of the true prairie that it can be called poor. A number of farms have already been located, which with improved methods of culture will, I doubt not, be found fairly remunerative.

Soon after we had pitched our tent on Saturday afternoon it began to rain, and continued to rain at intervals during the night and on the following day. Arrangements were made to hold service in the School House on Sunday evening, and at the appointed time I preached to an attentive congregation. Although the night was pitch dark, and walking very bad, the School House was well filled.

Monday forenoon was spent in " exploring " the ground, and collecting information. In this, as in other matters, I received much kind assistance from Mr. P. G. Laurie, the proprietor of the *Saskatchewan Herald,* a spirited little sheet, published once a fortnight, containing much useful information from various parts of the great North-West. During the forenoon the weather moderated, so we speedily got our effects together, and at 12 o'clock were ready to embark. Mr. Laurie kindly gave us permission to replenish our potato bag from his garden, and in the stores we found all that we required in the way of provisions. We pulled down Battle River, and in less than half an hour were again on the waters of the Saskatchewan. During the afternoon we made about 25 miles, and then went ashore for tea. Pulled on again till it was quite dark, when finding navigation difficult, on account of the many sandbars, we tied up and waited for day. Early in the night it began to rain, and next morning it was raining still. I quote from my journal :—

" *Tuesday, Aug. 13.*—Dull, heavy morning ; rain alternating with Scotch mist. Just why this wretched kind of weather should be called 'Scotch' I don't know ; but if this be the kind of mist that prevails in Scotland, that proverbially long-headed people 'missed' it badly when they made the investment. If any one is disposed to remark that he hardly ever heard a worse pun, let him try, under similar circumstances, (6 a. m.—cold, cheerless morning—drizzling rain—wet to the skin) to make a better. At Edmonton and other places we had been assured that we might confidently anticipate fair weather and good

10

roads during the latter half of August and the first half of September; but we seem, on the contrary, to have reached the very spot described by Longfellow where—

' It rains and the wind is *never* weary.'

We rowed hard, but the rain continued, and altogether we passed a rather uncomfortable day,—consoling ourselves as best we could, with the reflection that

' Into each life some rain must fall,
Some days must be dark and dreary ;'

though it seemed as if all the rain there was intended to fall during our trip down the Saskatchewan. Towards evening we pulled ashore, and, clearing a space among the bushes, pitched the tent, built a huge fire in front, got supper ready, dried our clothes, and cutting armsful of bushes, dried them over the fire and spread them on the damp ground in the tent as a foundation for bedding. Lay down about 9 p. m., thoroughly tired."

To our great delight, Wednesday morning, Sept. 1st, broke clear and cloudless, and the weather continued bright and pleasant all day. No time was lost in preparing breakfast, and we got away in good season. In about a couple of hours we reached the well-known "Elbow" of the North Saskatchewan. We had been told that from this point to Fort Carlton the distance was 40 miles, but we concluded it must be much greater, as we rowed hard all day, and at 6 p. m. the Fort was not yet in sight. Pulled two hours longer, but no Fort. As we did not want to pass it unawares in the darkness, we tied up for the night. At daylight the next morning we pushed off, and in about 20 minutes sighted the Fort in the distance. As we were now sure of our whereabouts, we stopped to breakfast, and then pulled to the landing. Soon after getting ashore, a courteous message was received from Lawrence Clarke, Esq., Chief Factor of the Lower Saskatchewan District, offering us the use of rooms at the Fort. He despatched a waggon to the boat to bring up our effects, and entertained us hospitably at dinner.

Meanwhile, our horses were brought in from the Company's "guard;" and about 2 p. m. I started, in company with Mr. Warren, for Prince Albert, while Mr. Steinhauer and Sam took the boat down the river. This took me some 50 miles out of my way, and these 50 miles had to be travelled back again before I could get on the direct road to Winnipeg; but I was very desirous of visiting the settlement, that I might test the correctness of certain reports that had reached me about the need for a Methodist Missionary at that point. About 6 p. m. we reached one of the first houses in the settlement, occupied by a young Scotchman, named Finlay. He has a "half-section" of land (320 acres), some stock, and the prospect of good crops. He came in some four or five years ago with $50, and now considers himself independent. He has a new house in course of erection, and altogether a promising future. As his present house had but one

room, we gladly accepted the use of his granary as a
shelter for the night, and spreading our blankets on the
floor, slept comfortably.

The next morning we drove on toward Prince
Albert.  The country, with the exception of a narrow
belt covered with fir, seemed admirably suited for
farming purposes.  There are numerous small lakes,
but no very great amount of waste land; and the
crops we saw in the fields, especially the wheat, seemed
of excellent quality and very abundant.  The season
—all unite in saying—has been exceptionally wet and
late.  It was now the 2nd September, and wheat
harvest was just beginning; but in some places we
found the crop had been damaged by the early frosts.
This, we were told, is a very unusual circumstance;
but I am not clear that the seasons in this region are
to be fully depended upon.  Still, it must be confessed the disadvantages in this respect are no greater
—if as great—than they were in some of the best parts
of Ontario 40 years ago.

About noon we reached the part of the settlement
to which we were bound.  Several villages have been
started at different points on the river, and it seems a
little doubtful which will ultimately take the lead.
The H. B. Company have laid out a town plot, which
they have named Goschen, and as it commands the best
landing from the river, and has large grist and saw
mills within its bounds, it is not unlikely it will be
able to hold its own against all competitors.  One
thing, however, may be regarded as certain : a town of

importance is sure to spring up somewhere about this point at no distant day.

About the middle of the afternoon, the boat containing Mr. Steinhauer and Sam arrived from Carlton. While we had taken a pretty straight course across the country, they had been obliged to follow the windings of the river, hence their journey occupied more time than ours. From the time we left Victoria, the Saskatchewan had been rising. During the past few days the rise had been very rapid, and now it was booming from bank to bank, a wide and muddy flood, covered with driftwood and foam. A Mr. McKay informed us he had lived 63 years in the neighborhood, and in all that time had never seen the Saskatchewan so high at this season of the year. The high water has enabled the Company's steamer to make several additional trips up the river—a great boon to those who have shipped goods by that route.

We had been informed that, although there was no regular hotel at Prince Albert, there was a house where comfortable meals could be obtained. This house, we found, was kept by a Mr. Deacon, who has two brothers in the ministry of the Methodist Church in Ontario. In the front yard we pitched our tent, which we used for sleeping purposes, while we obtained our meals in the house. Mr. Deacon seems to be pushing his way in the new settlement. He has a commodious brick hotel in course of erection, which in less than a year will furnish good accommodation to all travellers who may visit the place. I may remark that, as the sale of intoxicating liquors is prohibited in the North-West Territories, hotel-heeping in that country is free from the taint which attaches to it in the Provinces ; and hence the hotels are just what they ought to be,—places of accommodation for travellers —not resorts for tipplers. Heaven grant that the curse of strong drink may never blight these prairies of the West !

On Saturday, Mr. Deacon kindly placed his time at my disposal, and we drove into the country, visiting a number of Methodist families who have moved in from Ontario. There are also in the settlement quite a number of young men who were connected with the Methodist Church before coming here. All seemed very anxious that a cause should be established in the place, and assurances were given that if a man could be sent, a house would be provided for him to live in, and a place of worship erected with but little delay. I was also informed by some of these friends that they knew of other Methodist families who were on their way out from Ontario; and they were convinced, from careful inquiry, that a Missionary of our Church would find throughout the settlement, at the very outset, not less than a hundred hearers of Methodist proclivities.

A vacant store having been secured for the purpose, I preached on Sunday morning, on short notice, to a congregation of 26 persons. Old associations were revived, and I trust that lasting impressions were made. In the evening I preached in the Presbyterian church, by invitation of the pastor, and had a full and very attentive congregation. The Presbyterians were the pioneers, I believe, in this settlement, and are deserving of commendation for the work they have done; but in these rapidly-growing communities, no one denomination can long supply either the needs or the wishes of the people, and all the Protestant Churches of the Dominion must do their share in the evangelization of the great North-West.

The Anglicans have also established a cause at Prince Albert, and Bishop McLean has made this the headquarters of his diocese. He has erected a large frame-building, now approaching completion, which is called St. John's College, and has some half-dozen clergy associated with himself in the neighborhood. One wonders a little just what they all find to do; but I suppose a " Cathedral " couldn't well be run with a smaller number. When the good bishop was only a curate, he was regarded as decidedly evangelical, and very liberal withal; but since his elevation to the episcopate, he is much more disposed to view other denominations from the "street acquaintance" stand-point. Indeed, if report is to be trusted, he so magni-fies his office that he no longer describes events as having occurred *Anno Domini* so and so, but as having occurred so many years or months before or after "my consecration!" Well, I suppose all men—even good men—have their weaknesses, and we may be thankful that the hallucinations of our Anglican brethren are usually of so harmless a type.

## XV.

## PRINCE ALBERT TO TOUCHWOOD HILLS.

THE morning of Monday, September 6th, was bright and beautiful. We were up betimes to make arrangements for a start; but, as usual, a great many "last things" had to be done, so it was half-past nine before we were ready for the road. The river journey was ended, and we must again take to the plains; and as one team could not transport both passengers and baggage, some additional outfit had to be procured. After some inquiry I purchased, from a member of the police force, a native "Bichon" pony, for $55. In Mr. Deacon's yard stood a new cart, which a young man had brought when coming to the country and now wanted to sell. We soon came to terms at a moderate figure. A set of cart harness cost me some $7 more, and this completed the necessary outfit. Tent, camping outfit, and provisions were packed in the cart, and put in Sam's charge, the remaining passengers took the spring waggon and ponies that had come all the way from Fort Benton, and away we went, Mr. and Mrs. Deacon kindly accompanying us a few miles on our way.

On reaching the Anglican Church, about a mile from the starting-place, we stopped, and entering the little cemetery, stood for a few moments at the grave of the late E. W. Skinner. Some of my readers will re-member the circumstances of his tragic and untimely death. When a lad he spent several years in the North-West in the family of the late Rev. George McDougall. Some time after his return to Ontario he became the subject of that great spiritual change which often decides the destinies of men for this world as well as the next. As usual the change was followed by a burning desire that others might become partakers of like precious faith, and this ultimately deepened into a conviction that God had called him to preach the Gospel to the heathen. His mind turned to the North-West, and he offered for service among the Indians in that field. After consultation it was resolved to send him out as assistant to the Rev. John McDougall, that his qualifications might be tested in the vast field east of the Rocky Mountains, and under the watchful oversight of an experienced Missionary. Mr. Skinner set out accordingly for his distant sta-tion, going by way of Winnipeg. At the latter point he obtained the necessary outfit and supplies, and then pushed on to the West. For some distance across the plains he travelled in company with a small de tachment of Mounted Police ; but their disgusting profanity, especially that of the officer, become so unbearable, that he left them, and travelled the rest of the way with a single companion, a half-breed, whom he met with on the journey. When at a point about midway between Forts Carlton and Pitt they had camped for the night. In the morning the half-breed went after the horses, and Mr. Skinner proceeded to arrange his tent, &c., on the buckboard. No one saw what followed, but when the messenger returned with the horses, he found him lifeless by the side of the buckboard, shot through the heart. The half-breed thoroughly terrified, instantly mounted one of the horses, and, without touching the lifeless body, fled back to Fort Carlton and gave the alarm. A party of men were at once despatched to bring in the body ; but in the meantime an English gentleman, the Hon. Mr. Percy, came by, returning with several others from a hunting expedition to the Far West. He took careful note of all the surroundings, and his evidence at the inquest, subsequently held at Fort Carlton, made clear the way in which the accident had occurred. A double-barreled breech-loading gun lay across the seat of the buckboard, underneath some articles of baggage, with one barrel discharged ; the wound in the breast of the unfortunate young man, supposing the body to be in an upright position, was just on a level with the muzzle of the gun ; the glove of his left hand was torn and burnt by the discharge ; and hence the conviction seemed irresistible that he had seized the weapon with one hand to push it from

him, forgetting, perhaps, that it was loaded; that in
doing so one of the hammers struck violently against
the opposite arm of the seat, causing an instant discharge, with the fatal result already mentioned. The
body having been brought into Fort Carlton, an
inquest was held before Lawrence Clarke, Esq., J.P.,
when a verdict of accidental death was returned;
after which the remains were sent to Prince Albert
and interred in the Anglican burying-ground, in the
grave beside which we stood.

Proceeding about a mile farther, our kind friends
who had accompanied us thus far, bade us farewell,
and turned back to Prince Albert, leaving us fairly on
the way to Winnipeg, some 550 miles distant. Even
with good roads and fresh horses it would require a
full fortnight to make the distance; but with frequent
rains and horses already wearied, it was likely to take
us a good deal longer. But then we were "homeward
bound," and that was an inspiration, although the
home itself was yet 2,000 miles away. We followed
the regular trail toward Carlton for about 20 miles,
when we turned to the left and struck for the South
Saskatchewan, which we hoped to cross that night.
Much of the land appeared to be of excellent quality,
and the homesteads we passed gave promise of a good
harvest, especially of wheat and vegetables. At one
house by the wayside we procured a small bag of
potatoes and some excellent fresh butter, the former
at $1 a bushel, and the latter at 50 cents a pound.
Late in the afternoon we reached the river at a place

known as " Gortapee's Ferry ;" but the river was about
a mile wide, the scow was on the farther shore, and
our utmost lung power could not attract the ferryman's attention ; so we drove on toward Fisher's ferry,
some 15 miles up the river. Much of the land here-
abouts is a light sand, of little value. In the evening
we camped by a pool among some willows, where we
found abundance of excellent water.

Making an early start on Tuesday morning, we
reached Fisher's ferry about half-past seven ; but we
had some delay before we could get the ferryman and
his men to work. A party of Canadians had just
crossed on their way toward Prince Albert, and I
shrewdly suspect they had supplied the ferryman with
whisky, for he was just drunk enough to take things
easy, and to put off crossing as long as he could. I
judged him to be a French half-breed, as he spoke with
a French accent. When I saw the huge scow that was
to transport us over, I said,

" How do you manage this big affair ? "

" Oh," said he, with all the importance of a half
drunk man, " dere are two of *me !* "

Then it seemed to dawn upon him that he had'nt
got the thing just right, and with a further accession
of maudlin dignity he added, " Dere are two of *us !* "
The two proved to be four, but it needed them all, and
help from the passengers beside, to get the big clumsy
scow with its load over the rapid current. These
erries, I may remark, are licensed by the Dominion

authorities, and a tariff of charges is posted in a conspicuous place for the information of travellers.

By dint of persevering effort we got over by nine o'clock, and driving a few miles farther stopped for breakfast. I tried here to bargain with a French half-breed for a horse, but found it hard to keep him to the point. First he brought a horse I would'nt have taken as a gift, then he brought another, but higgled, like an Arab, about the price. Finally, I agreed to give him " seventy piastres " for the animal. Subsequently, when I was about to pay him, he insisted the price was to be seventeen pounds sterling (about $85). Of course I did not submit to this, and sent him to the right-about, sorry that I wasted so much time with the rascal. Resuming our journey, the trail took us up the river on the south side till we reached Gabrielle's ferry, when we turned south-easterly and struck out over the plain. The weather was good and the road dry, and we made as good progress as the somewhat tired condition of our horses would admit of. In the evening, as the sky was threatening, we camped behind a clump of poplar and willow. During the night a heavy thunder-storm passed by, of which we got a liberal share.

*Wednesday, Sept. 8th.*—The storm of last night has made the trail "greasy," and bad for the horses, who begin to show unmistakable signs of fatigue. I must exchange one or two, or procure fresh ones, at the earliest opportunity. About 3 p. m. to-day we struck the line of the Pacific telegraph, and felt a thrill of

delight at beholding this sign of advancing civilization.
A drive of 16 miles farther brought us to Humboldt,
the only telegraph station between Battleford and
Fort Pelly.   Humboldt consists of a small log-house in-
habited by the telegraph operator (a lady) and her
husband, who has the task assigned him of keeping a
certain portion of the line in repair.   From the time
we left Battleford I had been looking forward with
interest to the time when we would reach Humboldt.
I had now been from home over eleven weeks, and in
that time but two letters had reached me, the second
written only some ten days after I left Toronto.   But
I hoped to end uncertainty when I reached Humboldt,
by sending a telegram and waiting for a reply.   " Hope
told a flattering tale," however; for when the telegraph
station was reached behold the line was broken somewhere between that point and Fort Pelly !   The storm
of the previous night had blown down some of the
poles—so they said, and I thought the statement very
probable, for most of the poles we saw were poplar
saplings, that looked as though one could easily blow
them down with an average pair of bellows.   The disappointment was intense, but there was no remedy ;
so we chatted awhile with the inmates of the cabin,
with what grace we could muster, and then returned
to our camp.   At this point we overtook the Rev. A.
Whiteside, who was on his way to Winnipeg to meet
his wife.   We took him with us, as he had no other
means of travelling.

During Thursday we struck what is known as Big

Salt Plain, a vast, treeless space, with more or less alkali at intervals. Before leaving the poplar bluffs entirely behind us, we secured some dry wood, which we carried with us, as we were not likely to find any more till we reached the Touchwood Hills. The soil of this plain, although not of the best quality, I would not consider by any means entirely worthless; nor do I think the proportion of alkali is sufficiently great to prevent settlement in the future. Perhaps we saw it under exceptionally favorable circumstances, the abundant rainfall of the past summer having improved the water somewhat, and left an abundant supply in places where, in ordinary seasons, not a drop would be found. In certain seasons of the year, the roads across this plain must present a great hindrance to travel, especially with loaded teams. We crossed two or three very bad places, but with the exception of having to jump out at one spot to help the horses through an alkili bog, we met with no mishap. During most of Friday we could see the blue outlines of the Touchwood Hills in the distance; but in the intervening space not a tree or shrub could be seen to break the monotonous view. In the evening, however, we reached the timber bluffs, and camped by the side of a grassy lake.

At many points on our long route, wild duck had been seen in considerable numbers; but after we crossed the south branch of the Saskatchewan, it seemed as though we had reached the very paradise of sportsmen. The whole country through which we

travelled abounds in small grassy lakes, where wild
fowl find a congenial breeding place and home ; while
on some large lakes that we passed they swarmed by
tens of thousands.   Not a pond two rods wide did we
pass, but had a dozen or more splendid ducks floating
on its surface with a calmness that was positively
exasperating.   They seemed to be quite aware that we
had parted with  our only shot-gun, that  we had  no
dog, and that if we happened to  hit a stray duck with
the rifle,  we would not be  likely to wade  in through
the water and slush to get it ; and so they floated about
with  the  utmost  unconcern,  and  their  very  quack
seemed to have a note of interrogation in it, as though
they were asking—" Wouldn't you like to try a shot ?"

On Saturday  morning  a  dense  mist  covered  the
earth and hid the sky.   Showers fell at intervals, but
undeterred by the prospect, we broke camp and drove
on.   About  8 a.m.  we  passed  the  Government Instruction Farm, and talked for a few minutes with the
Instructor, a  Mr. Scott.  'The  scenery through  these
Touchwood Hills is  exceedingly beautiful  and park-
like.   The  poplar bluffs  are  numerous,  interspersed
with stretches of rolling prairie ; many small lakes lie
among the hills ; streams of pure water are frequently
met with ; and the whole forms as charming a  picture
as one need wish to see.   Much of  the land appears to
be of excellent  quality, and Mr.  Scott spoke in  high
terms of  the  portion already brought under  cultivation.   /

During the  forenoon,  as we were  driving  over  an

open stretch, a covey of prairie chickens were seen a
short distance ahead. As we had been out of fresh
meat for some time, I resolved to try my luck with
the rifle. My first shot was fired rather hastily, and
missed them all. At the next shot I was fortunate
enough to get three birds in line, and taking careful
aim, dropped the three at once, two shot through the
neck and one through the body. Three birds remained, and taking careful aim, I dropped them one
by one, cutting the neck in each instance. "Pretty
good shooting," says some captious reader; "but why
don't you tell us of the many shots fired during the
journey when you didn't hit anything?" "That
reminds me : A colored preacher was delivering a
sermon preparatory to the immersion of some converts
in the river. Addressing the crowd of onlookers, he
said,—' Now, I s'pose some o' you folks want to know
why immu'shon am de only Script'ral mode o' baptism? Laws bress you, brudderin; *it ain't none o' yo'
bis'ness!'*" After the manner of men who write
biography or autobiography, I have reported the suc-
cesses ; let some one else mention the failures.

Shortly before noon, we passed a house where we
met the mail-carrier going westward, accompanied by
the Rev. Mr. Pitblado, of Halifax, who was going as
far as Prince Albert. They reported the roads farther
east in a very bad condition, which implied the possibility of further delay to our party. As it was
necessary to obtain some fresh horses, as well as a
supply of provisions we pushed on to the H. B.

**11**

Company's post, which we reached before one o'clock, and pitched our tent in a grove of poplars, a few hundred yards from the Fort. During the afternoon, Mr. McKay, the officer in charge, sent out to the "guard" for a band of horses, from which we selected two that we thought would suit our purpose; but this consumed most of the afternoon, and we resolved to remain in camp till Monday. Heavy showers fell at intervals; the wind increased to a gale; and it became so cold that we expected a fall of snow before morning. During the night the wind at times approached a hurricane in violence; but as our tent had been pitched in the timber, we were sheltered from the worst of the storm.

## XVI.

## TOUCHWOOD HILLS TO BIRTLE.

EFORE daylight on Sunday, Sept. 12th, the
wind moderated, and early in the forenoon
the clouds dispersed and the sun shone out
brightly, while the temperature rose quickly
to moderate summer heat. On going out to
see that our horses were safe, we found that
my "Bichon," though securely "hobbled," had wan-
dered away during the night. As there was no telling
to what distance he might go, if let alone, a search
was instituted without delay. In the afternoon we
saw an Indian who said that some miles back on the
road we passed over yesterday, he had seen early in
the morning, a horse resembling the one we described.
We gave the Indian some food, and he agreed to go in
search of the missing animal; but up till evening no
tidings were received.

On Monday morning several Indians joined in the
search, and about 8 a.m. the missing horse was
brought back, having been found some two miles from

the camp. So far good. But just at this juncture the Indian in charge of the Company's horses at the "guard" arrived, saying that one of the animals we had purchased on Saturday could not be found. Here was a fresh dilemma. But neither grumbling nor scolding could do any good ; so I took Sam with me and started for the "guard." We found one of the horses all right, but the other was missing. The Indian was getting his breakfast in his tent, but immediately after was ready to resume the search. He started out on horseback, accompanied by Sam ; but an hour's search resulted in nothing, and they returned to the tent. Again the Indian started in a new direction, and in less than an hour came in with the missing horse. So we returned in triumph to camp, got some dinner, and at 2 p. m. were once more on the trail. Early in the day I had been purchasing some supplies at the H. B. Company's store, when Mrs. McKay, wife of the officer in charge, most kindly presented me with several loaves of delicious home-made bread ! If she did not receive in return " the blessing of him that was ready to perish," she received at least the fervent benediction of those who knew how to appreciate such a gift at such a time.

A couple of miles out we stopped to get some potatoes. We had been told of a farmer who would probably supply us, but we mistook the house, and stopped at a kind of store. The man had some potatoes already dug, which he poured from his bag into ours, after which they were weighed and paid for at the rate of $1.25 per bushel of 60 lbs. We subsequently discovered that we had got very inferior potatoes, including several pounds of *peelings.* I am sorry I did not get the name of the rascal, that other travellers might be warned; but those who are going West, and are in need of potatoes, had better deal with the owner of the *first* house they come to when approaching Touchwood Hills, or else wait till they get to the H B. Company's post, about two miles ahead.

On the 14th, we made pretty good progress through a piece of excellent country, bluffs of timber alternating with stretches of open prairie. On the following morning the ground was covered with hoar frost; and ice about one-eighth of an inch in thickness had formed on some water left in a pail. When leaving camp we took a supply of wood, as we had to cross Pheasant Plain, which is entirely destitute of timber. We found the road very good, with the exception of occasional sloughs and creeks, some of the latter so deep that the water came well up the waggon box. After crossing the last of these creeks, we camped for the night. Next morning, as our stock of wood was exhausted, we were astir at dawn, so as to reach a distant bluff in time for breakfast. Reaching the spot indicated, we "spelled" till 9 a. m. On again till 12, and halted for dinner. Shot a couple of prairie chickens with the rifle. Met several trains of carts, some going West with freight, and others carrying supplies for a number of surveying camps.

Speaking of this section of the country, Professor

BUFFALO SKIN LODGE AND RED RIVER CARTS.
From Grant's *Ocean to Ocean*, by permission of the publishers.]

Macoun observes :—" Pheasant Plain, which extends from the crossing of the Pelly Road eastward for 25 miles, is altogether without wood ; but the soil is exceedingly rich, and at no point is the wood to the south-west 10 miles distant. Proceeding northward of the travelled road, the country becomes more broken, ponds and marshes are numerous, and wood increases both in size and quantity until it merges into continuous forest south of the location of the Canadian Pacific Railway. A rich black loam, about 15 inches in depth, containing small grains of quartz or other rock, is the prevailing surface soil ; but this imperceptibly passes into lighter colored, sandy loam, as the timber becomes more continuous and of a larger growth. The subsoil is generally a light-colored, marly clay ; but this again, in the ridges, passes into gravel, which is generally gneiss covered with a coating of carbonate of lime. . . . . At many points we dug into the subsoil, and found it as above. Tested with acid, it always gave indications of a very large percentage of carbonate of lime."

Friday, Sept. 17th, I hailed as my natal day. Gladly would I have spent it at home, had that been possible ; but even " the wings of a dove " would not have sufficed to cross the space that separated me from those I held dear. During the forenoon we reached Cut Arm Creek; which we forded without trouble, but had a stiff pull up the steep hill on the eastern side. The scenery here is more varied than what we have been passing through for several days. At noon we halted near a grove, where in a valley we found springs of good water. In the afternoon we diverged from the trail leading to Fort Ellice, with the view of crossing the Assinaboine at a ferry some four miles above the Fort. In an hour or so we reached the banks of the Qu'Appelle River, where we looked upon one of the loveliest valleys we had seen during the entire trip. The banks descend abruptly from the level prairie for some 200 feet, and end in a level bottom about a mile wide. Through this valley the Qu'Appelle winds in graceful curves, bordered with rich pasture lands of considerable extent. The southern bank is covered with a fine growth of poplar, now yellow with the tints of approaching autumn.

It is the opinion of some that this valley once formed the outlet of what is now called the South Branch of the Saskatchewan. The theory does not seem improbable. It is almost certain that a much larger stream once flowed through the Qu'Appelle Valley than is to be found there at present. Then the course of the South Saskatchewan for a long distance is almost due east, and in a direct line towards the head of the Qu'Appelle Valley; but at a point which may be roughly described as Lat. 50 N., Long. 108 W., it turns sharply northward, and very near to this turn the head waters of the Qu'Appelle take their rise.

Following the north bank for some distance, and passing through groves of poplar and some scrub oak, we descended a succession of steep sand hills, and reached the Assinaboine at a point where a rope and scow ferry has been constructed, about four miles above Fort Ellice. The river is not wide and we crossed with but little delay. Ascending another long and steep bank we camped on the summit, thankful that we were over the last bridgeless river, and only about 200 miles from Winnipeg. In the evening we had a call from a French priest who had been out on the prairie looking for a stray horse. Early next morning he called again, and asked me to be the bearer of a letter to Pére Lacome, at Winnipeg. Of course I consented; but had he known who or what I was it was not likely he would have preferred the request.

Soon after breaking camp on Saturday morning, rain began to fall, which rendered our progress both slow and unpleasant. After crossing Snake Creek, we found another steep muddy hill, which took a long time to climb. About noon, looking down from the summit of a hill, we saw a cluster of houses in the valley, and in a short time found ourselves in the village of Birtle, cheered by signs of human habitations. The village is situated in a beautiful valley, on the banks of Birdtail Creek, a considerable stream of excellent water affording water-power to a large extent. A town plot of good size has been laid out by parties connected with the Hamilton Colonization Company. A saw-mill has been built, and is in operation. A number of houses have already been erected, and some 80 lots have been sold, all but three upon condition of being built on within a year.

As the day was cold and stormy we went into camp, resolved to remain till Monday morning. This gave great satisfaction to some Methodist families in the place, as they had been without a Missionary since last spring. All up and down the Creek for 35 miles, and eastward toward Shoal Lake, there are settlements, and the people are anxious for Gospel ordinances. There is a Presbyterian Missionary in the neighborhood, but among these widely-scattered settlements no one man can possibly supply the wants of the people. Since the Methodist Missionary left, an excellent Local Preacher, named Burritt, has been preaching with much acceptance ; but it is very desirable that a man fully set apart to the work of the ministry should be sent without delay. *

On Sunday morning a good congregation gathered in the house of a Mr. Lane, to which I preached with much comfort. In the afternoon, although the day was cold and disagreeable, the equinoctial storm having fairly set in, the large dining-room of Mr. McDougall's boarding-house was filled with a congregation mostly from Ontario, many of them Methodists, who listened attentively to the word spoken. In conversation afterwards, some of them expressed their earnest desire for a Missionary, and intimated their intention of uniting in the erection of a place of worship at an early date.

During our brief stay in Birtle we received much kindness from a Mr. Wood and his estimable family.

* A Missionary has since been sent.

Mr. Wood is from Woodstock, and is a prominent member of the Hamilton and North-west Colonization Company. During Saturday afternoon, in company with Mr Wood, I made a careful examination of the town plot, and selected a couple of lots as a site for a church and parsonage in the future. These lots are on a prominent corner, and together make a plot of 132 feet square. In this place I met several other acquaintances of former days—Mr. Balch, former editor of the St. Mary's *Argus*, now Land Agent at Birtle ; Mr. J. B. Carpenter, and others. Altogether the settlement is a most promising one, and those who have located farms here have made, I think, a good investment.

## XVII.

### BIRTLE TO PORTAGE LA PRAIRIE.

EFT Birtle on Monday morning, Sept. 10th, at 8 a.m. The storm has abated, but the weather is cold. The heavy rains have made the roads very "greasy," and travelling is slow. The storm and exposure have been too much for "Bichon," and he is quite sick to-day. We are passing through a fine prairie country,—rather low, perhaps, and with numerous ponds; but a considerable amount of good, rich soil. Mr. Marcus Smith, who explored this section of country in 1879, from Shell River to Birdtail Creek, speaks as follows :—" North of the Assinaboine the country rises gradually and imperceptibly to the eye up to the crown of the Riding Mountain, 2,000 feet above the level of the sea. The southern portion of this district is chiefly prairie; the soil good, but light in some places, and in others largely mixed with boulders. The depth of the soil increases northward, and its quality changes to a heavy loam, well suited for permanent wheat-growing; groves and belts of poplar become frequent, and ultimately merge into a solid forest, in which there are good spruce and tamarac."

To prevent confusion of thought in regard to the geographical position of this region, it may be necessary to remark that the Assinaboine River flows, for the first half of its course, in a southerly direction ; but some 20 or 30 miles south of the 50th parallel, it turns suddenly to the east, and holds an easterly course till it forms a junction with the Red River at Winnipeg. This will account for the fact that we crossed the stream from west to east near Fort Ellice, while Mr. Smith in the above extract, speaks of the country " north " of the Assinaboine.

At Shoal Lake we rested for a couple of hours, enjoyed a comfortable meal at a boarding-house (there are no " taverns " in the Territory, in the ordinary sense of the word), and then driving on for a couple of hours more, formed our camp on the prairie. Next day " Bichon " became so sick that it was evident he would not be able to go much farther. When about 25 miles from the Little Saskatchewan, I saw near the wayside the cabin of a settler. Driving over, I found the cabin was owned and occupied by a Mr. Griffith, from the County of Grey, who had moved in during the early summer. He cheerfully consented to let me leave my sick horse, promising to keep an eye on him in case he should get better. I had no expectation he would live 24 hours, but since then I have heard that he recovered ; still, as he has manifested a perverse disposition to wander off on the prairie, and has been lost several times, it is somewhat doubtful if I shall finally get the worth of him.

In the evening a somewhat early halt was called, as our stock of bread was exhausted, and it was necessary to make some more. As I have not yet described the process, it may be worth while to do so now. When making bread on the prairie, you may be said to work at a disadvantage, your apparatus being of the most limited kind. Of course we have a bag of flour and some baking powder; but now we must have a dish of some kind in which to mix them. A washbowl of granite ironware forms part of our outfit, but as that has been used for weeks, alternately in washing our faces and our potatoes, it does not seem just the thing to mix bread in. Fortunately, we have a spare tin dish, which, though small, will answer our purpose. Some flour, salt, and baking powder are thrown in, and sufficient water to reduce all to the proper consistency; and then we discover that we have no kneading-board. " Necessity," however, " is the mother of invention." The cart, standing near by has a tail-board, which, though still in the rough, and not much improved by its passage through sundry sloughs and creeks, presents, nevertheless, a solid foundation. This board Sam appropriates and in a very few minutes has his " bannocks " ready for the oven. Alas! we have no oven; but no matter. Sam seizes the frying-pan, throws in a bannock, tilts the pan at an angle of seventy degrees, facing the fire, rakes some glowing embers behind it, and in a wonderfully short space of time we have something which, if it would hardly pass inspection in a city bakery, is not to be despised by those who sit down to supper with a prairie appetite.

About 10 a.m. on Wednesday morning we reached Rapid City, on the Little Saskatchewan. For the last 12 or 15 miles, homesteads were visible on either side of the plain over which we had been travelling. At Rapid City we received a kindly welcome from the Rev. Thos. Lawson and his estimable wife. This is a fine section of country, and is being settled rapidly. The "city" contains some fifty houses, among which is the frame of a small church in course of erection. There are numerous stores and other places of business, and I should judge that considerable money changes hands in the course of the year. Mr. Lawson's Mission is large, and the settlements are widely scattered ; but with the assistance of a colleague, he is trying hard to meet the needs of the people. He occupies a small log house, adjoining which is a large garden, by the cultivation of which he tries to eke out a slender stipend.

In the afternoon we resumed our journey, intending to take the north trail some distance east of Rapid City. Bro. Lawson and his wife accompanied us, the latter going to her father's, on the Palestine Mission, the former proposing to accompany us as far as Portage la Prairie. But before evening, a horse which Mr. Lawson had hired to drive with his own " played out," so they camped with us for the night, and returned home the next morning.

Not having Mr. Lawson to guide us by the north trail, we resolved now to go by the south, with which Sam was quite familiar. Soon after breaking camp we entered Big Plain, a level stretch of prairie about 25 miles across. Much of this plain has been taken up, and homesteads could be seen in every direction as we passed along. The road was first-class, and had our horses been fresh we could have made splendid time. As it was, we reached the eastern side of the plain before evening, but finding no water we drove some distance farther, and found a good camping ground by the side of a fresh water lake.

Our route on Friday morning was over rolling sand-hills, with level prairie interspersed. After crossing Pine Creek we struck a beautiful piece of country, some of which is already brought under cultivation. In the afternoon we reached McKinnon's Woods, a place we had been hearing about for days, and which, when reached, realized our worst expectations. I have travelled bush roads in all parts of Ontario, but never struck a worse piece than this. We met numerous teams with emigrants on their way farther west, some of them looking discouraged enough " because of the way." I was glad to be able to cheer them with the assurance that it was " better farther on." Later in the day the clouds again began to " drop down fat-ness ; " but we had had so much of this kind of thing that we could have wished the clouds as lean as Pharaoh's kine, if that would have put an end to the drop-ping. Sometimes the sun would struggle through a rift, and the rain would cease, but before we had time to congratulate ourselves on the change, down it would come again. We were forcibly reminded of a worthy Scottish home missionary who was about to commence an out-door service, when a few drops of rain began to fall. Fearing that a shower would scatter his congregation, he devoutly lifted up his voice in prayer, asking that the Lord would be pleased to withhold the rain till the service was over, Even while he was speaking the rain ceased, and the worthy man's prayer was turned to praise; but e'er he had uttered a dozen words of thanksgiving, down came the rain again as though the bottom had fallen out. Opening his eyes, with a look of mingled astonishment and protest, the good man cried—" Eh, guid Lord, *this is perfetly rideeklous !*"

Plodding on through mud and mire, with what patience we might, we at last sighted a house near the wayside. This proved to be " Prangman's Hotel," and thankful for shelter for ourselves and our wearied horses, here we resolved to stay till the following morning.

On Saturday the roads for a number of miles were still very bad. It was no longer continuous bush, but stretches of low level prairie almost entirely covered with water. Sometimes to escape the "grease" and mud-holes on the trail, I would turn into the long grass where the horses had to wade through water almost up to their bellies for half a mile together. At one point the trail crossed a large pond—almost a lake

12

—that spread out for hundreds of yards in every direction. Just before were ached it, part of a company of Ontario emigrants had passed over, and entering the water from the farther side was a horse and cart, loaded with goods, on the top of which was perched a young couple who looked as though they belonged to one another or expected to do so shortly. But the course of their love did not run smoothly at this particular time, for when the horse reached the middle of the pond, he stopped, as if he had made up his mind to rest awhile; when the driver urged him with the whip, he made preparations to lie down. By this time we had reached the same part of the pond, and shouting at the unmannerly brute he became ashamed of his performance, and starting on took the young couple safely to the other side. Closing up the procession was a lad of 12 or 14 years of age, who crossed the water in triumph astride the back of a cow!

While "spelling out" at noon, Mr. McKenzie, of Rat Creek, passed by. He has an extensive farm on Big Plain, on which he had been working during the summer, and was now returning to his home at Rat Creek. He kindly invited us to call at his house on the way down. In the afternoon the roads improved somewhat, and it became evident we were approaching a better piece of country. Soon we reached the farms in the vicinity of Rat Creek, and saw fields of grain that would have delighted the heart of an Ontario farmer. A two hours' rest, and a cup of tea in Mr. McKenzie's hospitable home were much enjoyed.

Again we pushed on over a beautiful piece of country, cheered by the knowledge that we were within some nine or ten miles of the Portage. Our tired horses could go but slowly, however, and darkness came down before we reached our destination. At length the lights of the village began to gleam in the distance, and, almost feeling our way through the darkness, about half-past 9 p.m., on the evening of Saturday, September 25th, we turned into the yard of the parsonage at Portage la Prairie, where we received a cheery welcome from the Rev. W. J. Hewitt, Chairman of the District, and his excellent wife. The sense of rest and relief were inexpressibly delightful. Our toilsome journey across the plains was ended, and henceforth our way would be among the surroundings of civilization. No more boating down lonely rivers, under silent stars or dripping clouds; no more camping amid storms and cold, sleeping on grass saturated with rain, rising at dawn to search for wandering horses, or cook a cheerless breakfast; but pleasant homesteads, friendly faces, and comfortable resting-places everywhere and the iron horse but a few miles away, ready to speed us swiftly towards friends and home. Best of all a packet of letters from home, some of recent date, were awaiting me, and sitting up just long enough to gather from these that all was well, I gladly lay down to sleep.

## XVIII.

## PORTAGE LA PRAIRIE TO WINNIPEG, AND HOME.

EXT to Winnipeg, Portage La Prairie shows signs of more rapid and substantial growth than any other place in Manitoba. When I visited this point in the summer of 1877, there was but the beginning of a small village; now there is a goodly-sized town, containing the County buildings of Marquette, numerous stores, good hotels, several depots for agricultural implements and all kinds of carriages, a bank, mills, etc., etc.,—in short, everything that goes to make up a flourishing town. I found the business men a good deal exercised over the fact that the Pacific Railway was likely to pass some six miles to the north; but since then the route has been changed so as to touch the village, and the property-holders are happy. Whether the happiness will last is another question. Towns are not always made permanently prosperous by having a railway pass through them.

On reaching the Portage, I was pleased to meet the

Hon. J. W. Sifton, of Winnipeg, accompanied by the
Rev. James Scott, of Owen Sound. They had been
engaged for some time in a campaign through Marquette County in behalf of the Scott Act, and expected
to address a meeting at the Portage on Monday evening. On Sunday morning Bro. Scott preached a good
practical sermon, and a good class-meeting followed.
In the evening I preached to a full congregation.
The people are beginning to feel that the place is
too strait for them, and I have learned since my visit
that a more eligible site has been secured, and a temporary tabernacle built, preliminary to the erection of
a substantial church.

One of the first duties on Monday morning was to
despatch a message to Toronto, and in due time an
answer was returned, which removed all anxiety about
friends at home. The rest of the day was spent in
disposing of my horses and travelling outfit, which I
fortunately succeeded in doing at a less sacrifice than
I had anticipated. I was glad enough to dispose of
my waggon, tent, &c., but my noble little ponies, that
had accompanied me all the way from Fort Benton,
and throughout the whole journey had displayed so
much gentleness, pluck, and endurance, had come to
be regarded almost as personal friends ; and I confess
to feelings of genuine sorrow when called to part from
them. At noon I had the pleasure of dining with
Mr. Snyder, formerly of Eglington. He has a beautiful farm within two miles of the village, from
which he has reaped this year a magnificent wheat
harvest.

On Monday evening a meeting on behalf of the Scott
Act was held in a public hall of good size, which was
crowded to its utmost capacity. The Rev. W. J. Hewitt
presided, and capital speeches were delivered by Mr.
Sifton and Mr. Scott. Later in the evening I had the
pleasure of firing a shot in the same cause. During
the evening, a young man of fine appearance, but with
evident signs of dissipation, attempted to speak on
the other side. His appearance was greeted with loud
laughter, which waxed "fast and furious " as he went
on, "putting his foot in it," in the most absurd way,
at almost every sentence. Some were disposed to in-
terrupt him, but Bro. Scott quieted them with the
remark, "Let him go on; he's doing more for the
Scott Act than all the rest of us put together." I
afterwards learned that the young man was a tavern-
keeper ; that when he came to the Portage a few years
before he was both respectable and respected ; but like
many other young men in that country, he fell into
drinking habits, and now was almost constantly under
the influence of liquor. The poor fellow presented, in
his own case, an unanswerable argument for prohibi-
tory legislation.

Tuesday morning we started for a point some 20
miles from the Portage, where we expected to take
passage for Winnipeg by a construction train on the
Pacific Railway. Bro. Hewitt kindly took me along
in his buckboard, while the rest of the party went with
a hired conveyance. But travelling was now different
to what it had been. Instead of lonely plains stretch-

ing without sign of habitation far as the eye could reach, we now beheld, on every side, comfortable houses, neat fences, magnificent fields of wheat and oats, some of them fully 50 acres in extent, and all those other signs of a progressive civilization, so inexpressibly delightful after our long sojourn in the yet unpeopled regions of the farther west. Soon we reached High Bluff, where we stopped just long enough for a brief call on the Rev. J. M. Harrison, the Missionary there, who is succeeding well in his work ; then an hour's rest and a cup of tea at Mr. John Setter's, near Poplar Point ; after which we pushed on for the railway. About 5 p.m. we heard the cheering sound of the whistle, and ere long were on board the construction train, with all our remaining baggage, and by 6 o'clock were speeding eastward. At Meadow Lea we were joined by the Revs. J. G. Laird, and J. H. Starr, who had been making a brief summer visit to Manitoba, and at 10 p.m. reached the City of Winnipeg, and found quarters at a comfortable hotel.

On the next day the three chairmen of the Manitoba Districts met in the vestry of Grace Church, and we spent several hours in conversation concerning the work in the great North-West. The Methodist Church may well rejoice in the assurance that in regard to these honored brethren, we have " the right men in the right place." While vigorously pushing the work in the circuits of which they have charge, they are keeping a watchful eye on the ever-growing needs of the " regions beyond."

My time was now so limited that I could not spare an hour to visit the different parts of the city; but even a glance was sufficient to show what enormous strides Winnipeg has made in the past three or four years. Let the same rate of progress continue, and her growth will be as rapid as that of Chicago in its palmiest days. The chief danger is that real estate will run up to fabulous prices, and progress be crippled by individual greed. I am told that already on the main street as much as $12 per foot of frontage is paid as *ground rent* alone; and that a small corner lot, not on the main street, was lately sold for $13,000. It is doubtful if such prices can continue, and there may come, by-and-by, a "panic" in real estate that may retard the growth of the city for years.

Church enterprise in Winnipeg is by no means at a standstill. Most of the denominations are well represented, and have commodious buildings for so new a place. The Presbyterians have recently built a new and handsome church edifice, and the Methodist Church of Canada is preparing to follow suit. The latter body has two churches in the city at present— a commodious brick structure at Point Douglas, and Grace Church, on Main Street, which was built during the superintendency of the Rev. Dr. Young, and enlarged during that of the Rev. John F. German, M.A. The latter congregation have obtained a new site, and are preparing to erect a church which is expected to cost, when finished, not less than $30,000.

On Thursday morning, Sept. 30th., we crossed over

Red River to St. Boniface, and took the 8 a.m. train on the Pembina Branch of the Pacific Railway. The Rev. Dr. Young accompanied us as far as Emerson, where he is stationed at present. At Dominion City (not much of a "city" yet)—only three or four houses), we met the Rev. C. E. Blakeley, who is stationed at this point, and who is laboring diligently in his appointed field. The people are preparing to build a church, which is much needed. At Emerson we changed cars, and had some considerable delay passing baggage, &c. The town is some distance from the station, and we could not spare time to visit it; but Dr. Young reports it as a busy, prosperous place, and likely to be a point of considerable importance in the future.

On board the train I met Mr Cubbit, of Bacton Abbey, Norfolk, England, one of the English Farm Delegates who, at the request of the Dominion Government, had visited this country with a view to ascertaining its advantages as a field for immigration. Mr. Cubbit proved a most intelligent and agreeable fellow-traveller, and his views in regard to immigration were worthy of attention. Unfortunately the summer had been exceedingly wet, and Mr. Cubbit's visit to Manitoba had taken him through the muddiest roads in that muddy Province; hence he was not disposed to regard it in the most favorable light; but one could feel there was sound sense in the view that neither Manitoba nor the Western States was the place to which farmers of the class he represented would be likely to go,—men who were overseers and directors of labor, but who had never been trained to labor themselves. Neither did it seem to be the place to which to send the poorer class of English immigrants, people who had always been to a large extent dependent on others, and had but little self-reliance, or power to meet emergencies. At the same time Mr. Cubbit admitted that facts were rather against this latter view, as he had met in the older Provinces, especially Ontario, not a few who had been house or farm servants in England, and who, aided to Canada, in some instances by private or public charity, had worked their way to a manly independence. Men of large capital might do well; but why should men of large capital come at all? Men who had been accustomed to work, would doubtless succeed; but to send out families from the towns or maufacturing districts, people without means, and utterly ignorant of farm work, seemed like an act of positive cruelty; while the class of agricultural laborers, so long as they had the prospect of steady work, even at small wages, would be likely to cling to the old land. Some will think Mr. Cubbit's views rather one-sided; but it must be confessed they have considerable support from the history of immigration thus far.

I need not weary the reader by reference to any further incidents of the homeward journey. Suffice it to say that the rest of the trip was made without accident and without delay, and that at daylight, on the 3rd of October, I reached home, after some fifteen weeks of almost continuous travel, covering a distance, speaking roughly, of about 6,000 miles, 1,300 of which had been made by horses and waggon, and 700 by open boat, the rest by rail and steamer. The journey had been one of much fatigue and exposure, and at times of no small peril ; but through Divine goodness I returned in vigorous health, thankful that the object with which I set out had been fully accomplished.

## XIX.

### QUESTIONS ANSWERED.

N the preceding chapters I have adhered pretty closely to the narrative form, recording each day's doings and impressions as they arose. and hence I trust it will not be deemed out of place if I devote a concluding chapter to my impressions of the country as a whole, and to some matters which I could not well introduce at an earlier stage, without breaking the thread of the narrative. Perhaps I cannot fulfil my present purpose better than by throwing what I have to say into the form of answers to questions that have often been put to me since I returned from the North-West.

*" What is your opinion of the country ? "*

The question is very comprehensive, and would require, for a full answer, more space than I can give here. There are a few points, however, that may be briefly presented :—

1. It is a country of enormous extent. This can be realized fully only by one who has travelled through it. Figures may be piled up, and you may state the

area in acres or square miles; but such figures convey no very definite idea to the mind. The country, as you traverse the vast plains, becomes monotonous from its sheer immensity. If we take the distance west from Winnipeg at 800 miles, and the depth of the fertile belt between the boundary line and the North Saskatchewan at 200 miles (a moderate estimate), we have in that space alone an area of one hundred and sixty thousand square miles. And this does not take into account the enormous region known as the Peace River District, which will yet support a vast population.

2. It is a country of great fertility. One only needs to travel through it, noting the quality of the soil, the luxuriant growth of grass and vetches, and the fields of grain and vegetables where cultivation has been tried, to be convinced of that fact. The great drawback in many parts will be the scarcity of timber, but barbed wire will come into almost universal use for fencing; stone for building purposes will be found in some regions, and brick will be manufactured in others; the railways will bring in such supplies of lumber as may be required, while the vast deposits of coal in the Souris River country and farther west, will solve the question of fuel supply. On the whole I consider that we have in the North-West as fair a heritage as ever fell to the lot of any people.

" *What about the climate ?* "

It is much better than has often been reported. As a rule, the rainy seasons are well defined, and the amount of rainfall is not greater than the country needs. The winters are cold, judging from thermometer records, but the atmosphere is dry, the temperature steady, (none of those sudden and extreme changes so common in Ontario), and the people—even invalids—seem to suffer less from the climate than they do in the older Provinces. The snowfall is less, as a rule, than in Minnesota, Dakota, and Montana, and from all the information I can gather, I am inclined to believe the climate is better, on the whole, than in the states and territories just mentioned.

" *Why, then, do we receive so many unfavorable reports about the country ?* "

Chiefly because of the sources from which these reports come. Often they originate with Americans, who are interested in the sale of lands in Dakota and elsewhere. These men are to be found on almost every train carrying emigrants to the North-west, and they are by no means particular as to the statements they make if they can only induce Canadians to settle under the Stars and Stripes. They represent the North-West as a region so cold that nothing will ripen, and so unhealthy that nothing can live ; and not unfrequently Canadians are deterred by these disinterested (?) representations from entering the country at all, and report back to their friends that the North-West is not fit to live in.

Then, again, reports of this kind are sometimes set in motion by political partizans for political purposes—men who care little what injury they inflict upon the

country if they can only score a point against the opposite party. Those familiar with the Pacific Railway
debates of the last few years will need no other evidence upon this point.

But it will be said, not a few people who have
gone to the North-West with the intention of settling
there, have come away discouraged, and have brought
up "an evil report" upon the land. True, and for a
very simple reason: Most people enter the North-West
by way of Emerson and Winnipeg, and from these
points go westward for a short distance; they usually
go in early summer, the season of heavy rains, when
the roads are at the worst. Then Manitoba is the
lowest and flattest part of the whole North-West, and
consequently the part where travelling in the rainy
season is the most unpleasant. Going west from
Winnipeg towards Portage la Prairie, the traveller has
to pass over an exceedingly bad piece of road, of considerable extent ; then beyond the Portage, if his
courage has not given out, he finds on the north trail
at Palestine, or on the south trail at McKinnon's
Woods, as horrible a piece of country as he would
be likely to discover in a year of travel. Floundering
in mud and water below, and drenched by rain from
above, the man who has been accustomed in Ontario
to gravelled roads and comfortable stopping-places,
becomes utterly disgusted ; *he thinks this is a fair
specimen of the whole country*, and so he goes back and
reports that the whole thing is a fraud, and that he
wouldn't take a farm there as a gift. These are the

people, as a rule, who have brought back discouraging accounts of the country ; but during my whole trip I did not meet a single person who had been two years in the country, and who had gone manfully to work, who had the least idea of going back to Ontario, much less to the territory of Brother Jonathan.

*" Would you advise me to pull up stakes, and go to the North-West ? "*

That depends on circumstances. If you are doing fairly well where you are, stay there ; it is not worth your while to move for the sake of moving, or for the bare chance of doing a little better than you are doing now. In the next place don't go out with the idea of speculating in land ; there are too many speculators there now, and they are the curse of the country. Don't go out with the idea that you can pick up a living somehow without working,—there are no such livings to pick up. But if you are beginning life, and want a chance to become the owner of your own broad acres, owing no man anything, you can find as good opportunity in the North-West as in any land beneath the sun. If you have money enough to pay your passage, buy your quarter section, build your cabin, purchase enough stock and implements for present needs, and provide food till your first harvest is reaped, there is no good reason why your career in the North-West should not be one of steadily-growing comfort and prosperity.

*" What will be the future of the North-West ? "*

That will depend largely upon three things : 1. The

class of emigrants. 2. The character of the government. 3. The activity of the churches.

. Whence will come the population of the future? The question is pertinent at the present time when a scheme is being discussed for transplanting (I had almost said transporting) to the North-West the disaffected and poverty-stricken thousands of Ireland. Immigration of the sturdy and industrious classes of Ulster would doubtless be a valuable acquisition to our population; but these we are not likely to get in any great numbers; and immigration of the class proposed will be a very doubtful gain. We want no Biddulph neighborhoods in the North-West, nor neighborhoods where a Biddulph tragedy would be possible; yet these we shall have should the scheme now proposed prevail. There are no indications at present that we are likely to have any large influx from Scotland, or even from England, and hence we must look to Continental Europe as a base of supply. From Europe will come cheifly Germans and Scandinavians, the former largely imbued with Socialistic ideas, regarding monarchy and tyranny as interchangeable terms, and neither class having much faith in the Chrstian Revelation or the Christian Sabbath. Such elements are not easily fused into a strong homogeneous nationality.

The character of the government will have much to do with the future of the North-West. That it will make any serious difference whether the reins are held by the Conservatives or Reformers, no one but machine

13

politicians and their dupes are foolish enough to believe, for no great issues now divide the parties ; but
if the bitter and senseless party strifes of these older
provinces are to be carried into the North-West, the
same results will follow there that have followed here;
the very best men will scorn to enter the political
arena ; a large portion of the people will be unrepre-
sented in the government of the day ; the finances of
the country will be squandered, and its resources regarded but as a carcase around which the party eagles
may gather.   Perhaps it is expecting too much, but I
cannot willingly relinquish the hope that a day may
come when the best men of all parties will unite for
the common good, and, sinking party prejudices and
party bitterness, join their calmest counsels and best
efforts to pave the country's way to a future of prosperity and peace.

But whatever the population at the start, and whatever the government, Christian activity will be the
great factor in deciding the destinies of that vast
country.   If the great evangelical churches of this land
work diligently and wisely, not in building up their
respective denominational interests merely, but in
spreading broadly among the people the principles of
New Testament Christianity—love to God and good
will to men,—the problem will be solved, and the
foundations of empire will rest upon a basis that time
and change will be powerless to overthrow.   True,
there are dangers ahead,—and what country is without them ?   Avarice may build up huge monopolies,

party strifes may endanger great public interests, and the liquor traffic may distil its Upas poison over a domain that, as yet, is free from its deadly spell ; but on the other hand we start on the career of empire with no heavy burdens to carry, no huge abuses such as have grown up through centuries of ignorance and misgovernment in the empires of the old world, and no dark curse of slavery hanging like the shadow of doom above our national life. The future is bright with hope, and the course is open for a career that shall be ever " onward and upward." " May no Marius ever sit among the ruins of a promise so fair !"

As I pen these lines I stand again in fancy where a few months ago I stood in fact, on the summit of a lofty foot-hill of the Rocky Mountains. Behind me rose the mountain range, beyond which the sun was sinking toward the western sea, and I thought of the vast treasures embedded in those rocky fastnesses, which the hand of human enterprise would one day bring to light ; of the towering forests on the western slopes, vast enough to supply the markets of the world ; of the teeming fisheries with food supply for a continent, and fertile valleys where millions would yet find a home. Before me stretched the rolling foot-hills, and beyond these the distant plain ; but imagination passed swiftly onward to where the Atlantic surf breaks on our eastern coast, and I thought of the splendid harbors, and rich fisheries, and mineral wealth of Nova Scotia, the fertile acres of Prince Edward, the pine forests of New Brunswick, the commerce of

Quebec, the agricultural wealth and growing manu-
factures of Ontario ; of our mighty lakes, those high-
ways of commerce, that link together the East and the
West ; and then again my eye rested upon the varied
panorama of hill and vale and distant plain spread out
at my feet.   Far as the eye could reach there was no
sign of human habitation, and no sound of human activities broke the stillness ; but as thought took in the
possibilities of the future I stood intently  listening
like one who—

> " Hears from afar the muffled tread
>    Of millions yet to be,—
> The first low dash of waves where yet
>    Shall roll the human sea."

In fancy's ear I heard the lowing of cattle from the
hillsides, the hum of busy industry from a hundred
towns and villages, the  merry shout of children returning from school, and in the distance the thunder-
ing tread of  the iron horse as he sped swiftly across
the plain.   As I looked again the whole scene was
transfigured.   Everywhere quiet homesteads dotted
the plains and nestled among the hills, smoke of
factories rose thickly on the air, a hundred village spires
glittered in the rays of the setting sun, while golden
fields of ripening grain filled up the inter-spaces, and
waved in the passing breeze ; and I said in my heart,
" Lo, here  is a dominion stretching ' from sea to sea
and from the river unto the  ends of the earth ;' with
the garnered experience of the centuries behind it ;

with no fetters of past abuses to cramp its energies or
hinder its development; with no outside jealousies
ready to take advantage of its weakness, or avaricious
· neighbor covetous of its wealth.   Starting thus in
the career of empire with unfettered limbs, and a
hearty 'God speed' from the great sisterhood of nations,
surely nothing short of persistent folly or deliberate
wickedness can mar the future of its hopes."

" Fair land of peace ! To Britain's rule and throne
  Adherent still, yet happier than alone,
  And free as happy, and as brave as free ;
  Proud are thy children,—justly proud of thee.

" Thou hast no streams renowned in classic lore,
  No vales where fabled heroes roved of yore,
  No hills where Poesy enraptured stood,
  No mythic fountains, no enchanted wood ;
  But unadorned, rough, cold and often stern,
  The careless eye to other lands might turn,
  And seek, where nature's bloom is more intense,
  Softer delights to charm the eye of sense.

\*       \*       \*       \*

" We cannot boast those skies of milder ray,
  'Neath which the orange mellows day by day ;
  Where the magnolia spreads her snowy flowers,
  And nature revels in perennial bowers;—
  Here winter holds his long and solemn reign,
  And madly sweeps the desolated plain;
  But Health and Vigor hail the wintry strife
  In all the buoyant glow of happy life ;
  And, by the blazing chimney's cheerful hearth,
  Smile at the blast 'mid songs and household mirth.

" Here Freedom looks o'er all these broad domains,
And hears no heavy clank of servile chains;
Here man, no matter what his skin may be,
Can stand erect and proudly say 'I'M FREE!'
No crouching slaves cower in our busy marts
With straining eyes and anguish-riven hearts.

\*　　\*　　\*　　\*　　\*

" Fair land of peace! O may'st thou ever be,
Even as now, the land of LIBERTY!
Treading serenely thy bright upward road,
Honored of nations and approved of God;
On thy fair front emblazoned, clear and bright,—
FREEDOM, FRATERNITY, AND EQUAL RIGHT!"

PRINTED AT THE METHODIST BOOK AND PUBLISHING HOUSE,
78 AND 80 KING STREET EAST, TORONTO.